MUSHROOMS
AND OTHER FUNGI

BRIAN SPOONER AND THOMAS LAESSØE

HAMLYN

HOW TO USE THIS BOOK

This guide covers over 170 species of fungus, most of which are found in the UK. In the identification pages (42–125), they are listed broadly by family, although some unrelated species may be grouped together. The text gives an English name for each species (the commonest, wherever possible), the Latin name in italics, the average height (H), and other dimensions such as width (W), cap width (CW), stem width (SW) and stem length (SL). Abbreviated additional information is listed at the end of each description. Fr 4–6 shows the fruiting time, with the numbers 1–12 corresponding to the months of the year (eg. 4 = April). Usual habitats are then listed (see key 1), followed by the kind of substrate that the fungus actually grows on (key 2). The symbols positioned beside each illustration indicate how edible or poisonous that species is (key 3).

Key 1 – habitat

CWd = coniferous woodland
D = dunes
DWd = deciduous woodland
G = improved grassland
H = hedgerow
Hl = heathland
M = marsh and bog
Md = meadow
P = parks and gardens
PE = path edges
W = wasteland
Wd = woodland

Key 2 – substrate

B = burnt ground
Dg = dung
L = vegetable litter
M = moss
S = soil
W = wood
Mn = manure

Key 3 – edibility

Edible
Inedible or not recommended
Poisonous
Very poisonous

SLIMY SWAMPLING
Pholiota myosotis
H 10–20cm, CW 1–3cm, SW 2–4mm. Cap slimy, olive-brown, with whitish veil remains at edge. Frequent. Fr 8–10; M; M.

Editor: Julia Gorton
Series designer: Nick Leggett
Designers: Sarah Castell and Mei Lim
Picture researcher: Christine Rista
Production controller: Linda Spillane

Published in 1992
by Hamlyn Children's Books,
part of Reed International Books,
Michelin House, 81 Fulham Road,
London SW3 6RB

Copyright © 1992 Reed International Books Ltd
All rights reserved. No part of this publication may be reproduced, stored in a retrieval system, or transmitted, in any form or by any means, electronic, mechanical, photocopying, recording or otherwise, without the prior permission of copyright holders.

ISBN 0 600 57378 8

Printed in Hong Kong

SAFETY CODE

- SOME FUNGI ARE EXTREMELY POISONOUS – NEVER EAT ANY PART OF ANY FUNGUS UNLESS YOU HAVE CHECKED WITH AN EXPERIENCED ADULT TO MAKE SURE THAT YOU HAVE IDENTIFIED IT CORRECTLY

- ALWAYS WASH YOUR HANDS AFTER HANDLING FUNGI. IF POSSIBLE, TRY TO WEAR PROTECTIVE GLOVES WHEN HANDLING FUNGI THAT YOU KNOW TO BE POISONOUS

- DO NOT EAT ANY EDIBLE FUNGUS THAT HAS BEEN MIXED UP WITH OTHER POISONOUS SPECIES IN YOUR COLLECTING BASKET – WHEN YOU HAVE FINISHED EXAMINING THEM, THROW THE WHOLE LOT AWAY

CONTENTS

WHAT ARE FUNGI? · 4
CLASSIFICATION · 6
ECOLOGY OF FUNGI · 8
FINDING FUNGI · 10
EQUIPMENT AND COLLECTING · 12
LITERATURE AND IDENTIFICATION · 14
EDIBLE OR POISONOUS? · 16
CONSERVATION · 18
FUNGI AND MAN · 20
HABITATS:
   Gardens and Parks · 22
   Bogs and Swamps · 24
   Meadows and Pasture · 26
   Burnt Ground · 28
   Dung · 30
   Pine Woodland · 32
   Spruce-larch Woodland · 34
   Deciduous Woodland 1 · 36
   Deciduous Woodland 2 · 38
   Dunes and Heathland · 40
IDENTIFICATION · 42
Index · 126
Acknowledgements · 128

WHAT ARE FUNGI?

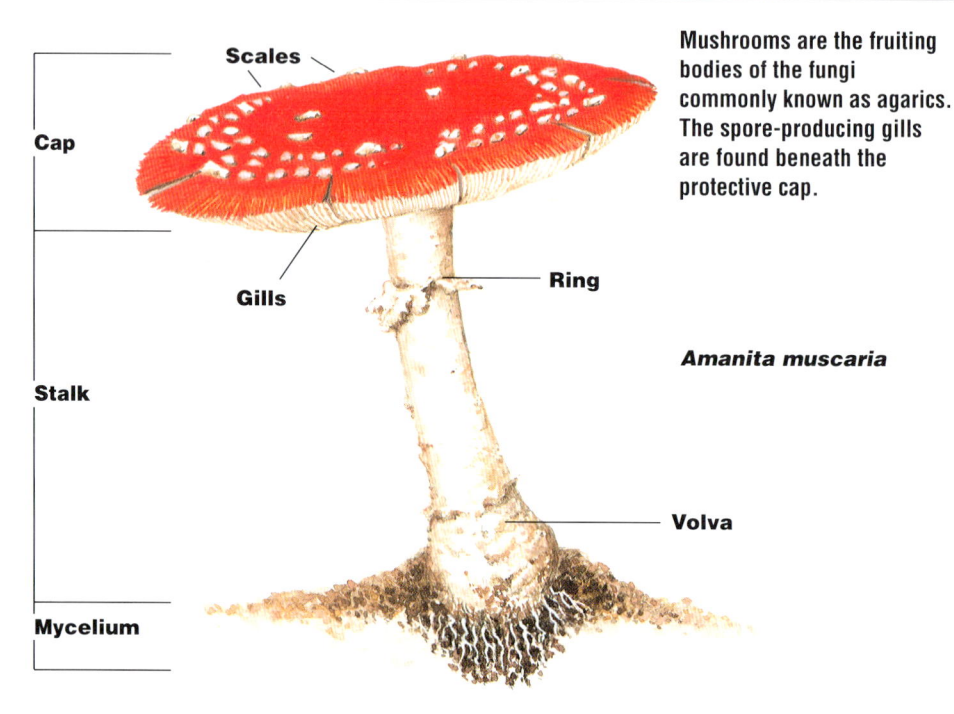

Scales
Cap
Gills
Ring
Stalk
Volva
Mycelium

Mushrooms are the fruiting bodies of the fungi commonly known as agarics. The spore-producing gills are found beneath the protective cap.

Amanita muscaria

The group of living things known as fungi includes puffballs, cup fungi, moulds, mildews, rusts and smuts, as well as the more familiar mushrooms and toadstools or gill fungi. All of these look very different, but their basic construction is, in fact, the same. They consist of microscopic, thread-like structures called hyphae, which branch to form a web, called the mycelium. The mycelium is usually hidden – perhaps under the soil, or within decaying wood. The part of the fungus that we actually see – a mushroom or toadstool, for example – is really only the fruiting body, like the flowers and fruit of a plant. The fruiting body produces the fungus's 'seeds' – masses of tiny spores, usually too small for us to see individually. One of the main ways that fungi are classified into different groups is according to the detailed structure of the parts that produce these spores.

Fungi occur in a wide variety of habitats, with different species being adapted to different environments. Their mycelium can commonly be found in soil, sand or leaf litter or, as shown here, on rotten wood.

STRUCTURE

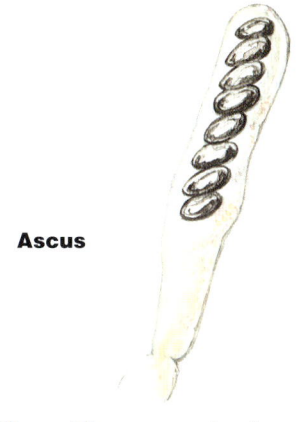

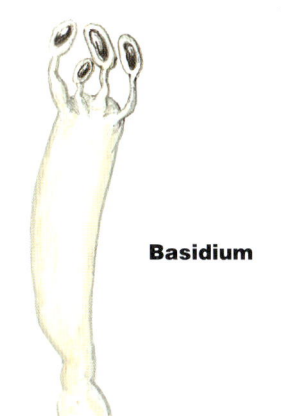

Ascus　　　　　**Basidium**

Two main kinds of spore-bearing structures are found in larger fungi. The spores of cup fungi and flask fungi develop inside sac-like structures called *asci*. Those of toadstools, brackets and relatives grow from club-shaped *basidia*, on tiny horn-like structures called *sterigmata*. Other kinds of spore-producing organs exist in mould-like fungi.

Many of the ascomycetes – the fungi that produce their spores in asci – have cup-or saucer-shaped fruitbodies. This kind of fruitbody is called an *apothecium*. In the *Otidea* shown here, the apothecium is very often split down one side, making it look like an ear. For this reason, the fungus is known as 'hare's ear'.

The fungi that produce their spores in basidia – the basidiomycetes – show a great range of different shapes amongst their fruitbodies. Toadstools are perhaps the most familiar, although the bracket-like fruitbody shown here is also a common example. There are many different kinds of brackets. Some are hard or tough and leathery, but others may be soft or fragile.

CLASSIFICATION

DIVISION

SLIME MOULDS
Division *Mycetozoa*
Not true fungi. Feed in the same way as amoebae. Spores powdery when mature.

FUNGI
Division *Eumycota*
The so-called true fungi. Formed of thread-like hyphae.

SUBDIVISION

'PHYCOMYCETES'
Subdivisions *Mastigomycotina* & *Zygomycotina*
Simplest fungi – includes some moulds and mildews.

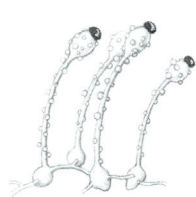

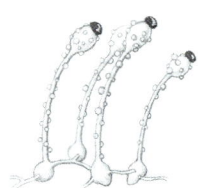

TRUE YEASTS
Subdivision *Saccharomycotina*
Single-celled fungi. Some used in food manufacture.

Subdivision *Basidiomycotina*

Subdivision *Ascomycotina*

RUST AND SMUT FUNGI
Orders *Uredinales* & *Ustilaginales*
Plant parasites with two or more different spore kinds.

JELLY FUNGI
Orders *Tremellales*, *Dacrymycetales* & *Auriculariales*
Basidia with dividing walls or shaped like tuning-forks.

STINKHORNS
Order *Phallales*
Fruitbody develops from jelly-like 'egg'.

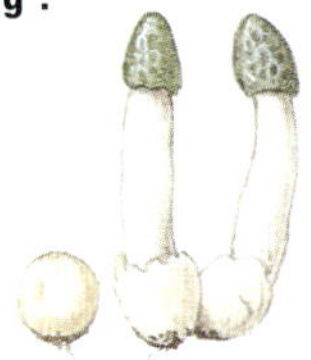

WITCHES' BROOM FUNGI
Order *Taphrinales*
Plant parasites, many causing galls. Asci form a layer on living leaves.

POWDERY MILDEWS
Order *Erysiphales*
Plant parasites. Fruitbodies closed. Asci rounded.

ORDER	FAMILY

POLYPORES
Order *Poriales* & allies
Often bracket-like. Spores formed in tubes.

SKIN FUNGI
Order *Stereales* & allies
Fruitbodies skin-like or similar to brackets.

Orders *Cantharellales*, *Gomphales* & *Hericiales*

MUSHROOMS AND TOADSTOOLS
Order *Agaricales*, *Russulales* & *Boletales*
Typical toadstools, with a cap and gills or tubes.

PUFFBALLS, EARTHBALLS AND BIRD'S NEST FUNGI
Orders *Lycoperdales*, *Sclerodermatales* & *Nidulariales*
Closed fruitbodies, with spores powdery when mature, or in 'eggs' within tiny 'cups'.

CUP FUNGI
Orders *Pezizales*, *Leotiales* & allies
Spore-producing sacs form a layer over exposed surface.

FLASK FUNGI
Orders *Sphaeriales*, *Dothideales* & allies
Fruitbodies usually shaped like flasks.

HEDGEHOG FUNGI
Families *Auriscalpiaceae*, *Hericiaceae* & *Hydnaceae*
Spore-producing surface on teeth or spines.

CHANTERELLES AND FAIRY CLUBS
Families *Cantharellaceae*, *Clavariaceae* & allies
Spore-producing surface on veins or ridges under cap, or on upper part of club.

FUNGI CLASSIFICATION

Fungi represent a separate kingdom of living things and should not be regarded as either plants or animals. There are many thousands of different kinds, showing a huge variety of shape and lifestyle, and their classification is still not fully settled even today. The fungus kingdom is split first into two divisions – slime moulds or *Mycetozoa* (not covered in this book) and the true fungi, or *Eumycota*. The true fungi are then grouped into five sub-divisions according to their method of spore production as well as details of their structure. The so-called larger fungi represent just two of these sub-divisions; *Ascomycotina* and *Basidiomycotina*. In Europe, these groups together include about 15,000 species.

ECOLOGY OF FUNGI

Unlike plants, which can make their own food using a special substance called chlorophyll and the energy from sunlight, fungi have to get the food they need from other organisms. Some obtain nutrients from living things, others thrive on dead plant or animal matter. Parasitic fungi, such as rusts, smuts and mildews, as well as many of the larger fungi, grow directly on a living plant or animal (the host), taking nutrients but giving nothing in return. Other fungi, including many of the woodland toadstools, take food in the form of sugars from for example, a living tree, but provide it with water and minerals in return. This takes place via the tree roots, and is known as a mycorrhizal association. Fungi that live on dead organic matter are known as saprobes. Many occur only on wood, others on fallen leaves or in humus. The species of fungi shown here are all found with birch trees.

Saprobes
Fawn pluteus (*below right*) grows on dead, rotting logs of birch as well as on other deciduous trees. Common leaf-disc (*below*) is one of several tiny cup fungi which grow, often in groups, on rotting leaves.

Mycorrhiza formers
Both brown roll-rim (*above*) and fly agaric (*left*) live in mycorrhizal association with birch trees. Below ground, the mycelium of each fungus is woven around the tips of the tree roots.

Parasites
Birch polypore (*right*) grows on birch trees which are stressed or weakened. The tiny yellow or orange spots of birch rust (*above*) can be found on both sides of living birch leaves.

FINDING FUNGI

Fungi can be found in all types of habitats, and even casual searching in a garden or local park will reveal a variety of species. Most fungi are specially adapted to live in one particular habitat or another. A fly agaric, for example, can be found only under birches or conifers. Many species are associated with trees or grow on wood, so woodlands are generally the best hunting grounds. It is also worth noting that many fungi are seasonal in appearance, fruiting only at certain times of the year. Although a range of species can be found in spring, the best season for fungus 'forays', as they are called, is in the autumn. All fungi require moisture to grow and develop, and a dry year can severely affect the numbers of fleshy fungi.

Specialised parasitic fungi can be found on a huge variety of different hosts and substrates. The tiny black dots on this flower bud, for example, are actually the fruitbodies of bud blast of rhododendron (*Pycnostysanus azaleae*).

HOW TO LOOK FOR SMALLER FUNGI

To successfully find the many tiny, and easily-overlooked, fungi which exist, you have to look closely at the substrate on which they grow. Examine fallen trunks and branches carefully, and look amongst rotting stems and leaves. Check the base of dead herb stems rather than the dryer, upper parts. If you do find something, a hand-lens is useful for a closer inspection.

Green-stained wood, ▷ which is commonly found in the litter of oak woods in particular, is caused by the mycelium of green wood-cup (*Chlorosplenium aeruginascens*). This fungus develops cup-shaped fruitbodies in the autumn. These are bright blue-green when they first appear.

▼ Several different species of small fungi grow commonly on fallen, rotting beechmast. The wiry, blackish fruitbodies of *Xylaria carpophila* are so specialised that they only grow on this substrate.

Amongst the leaf litter in ▲ oak woods, you may well find acorns that are blackened and wrinkled. These are infected by *Ciboria batschiana*, a cup fungus which fruits in the autumn.

EQUIPMENT AND COLLECTING

A selection of the most useful items needed for collecting fungi is shown here. A basket or box is much better than a plastic bag for carrying specimens.

EQUIPMENT AND COLLECTING

Only two pieces of equipment are really essential for a successful foray: a strong, flat-bottomed basket or 'trug', and a sharp knife (a safety knife with a locking blade is recommended). There are, however, several other items which you might want to take along – a trowel for digging out the stem bases of toadstools (to ensure that you have all possible clues to help with identification), a compartmented container such as a tackle box for storing smaller fungi, and a hand-lens for examining tiny details are all useful extras. It is also a good idea to have a notebook and pen with you for recording details of your finds.

A sharp knife is extremely useful on a foray, especially when collecting fungi growing on wood and other hard substrates. Several kinds of safety knives are available, and they are much safer than ordinary penknives.

You can photograph fungi in a way that can be very useful for identification. Lay several fresh specimens out so that all the characters of the species can be seen, as illustrated here with the death cap. Try to show the spore-bearing surface of at least one specimen, and include fruitbodies at different stages of development if available. For agarics, you could also cut one through to show the flesh colour and the way that the gills are attached.

PROJECT

Any species of *Amanita* is a good example of what a 'typical' toadstool looks like. You must handle these toadstools with extreme care, however, since this group includes dangerously poisonous species such as the death cap. Wear protective gloves for this project, and make sure that you wash your hands thoroughly once you have collected your specimen.

A small trowel is best for digging out this kind of fungus, although the blade of a knife can be used if necessary. Remove the soil and litter carefully to expose the base of the toadstool. Next, cut beneath it, making sure that you cause only minimal damage to the mycelium in the soil. Your complete *Amanita* specimen can then be lifted out intact and placed in your collecting basket.

LITERATURE & IDENTIFICATION

Many fungi can only be correctly identified once their basic characters have been carefully noted. Some of these need to be observed before the fungi are brought home for further study. These include notes on habitat and substrate (what the fungus is actually growing on ie. soil, wood, dung etc.) and on characters such as smell and colour. Other details to examine on fresh material are noted opposite. It is interesting and helpful to carry a field guide with you – it may even be possible to identify your specimen there and then. However, no single guide includes all species, and it is far more likely that you will need to refer to several books back at home to correctly identify a basketful of specimens. Various books should be available in your local library, although you may well want to buy one or two guides for yourself.

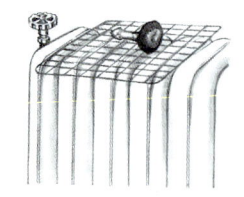

To preserve fungi, dry them over a radiator or similar source of heat, allowing warm, dry air to flow around them. This does destroy many of the fresh characters noted opposite, but it will preserve microscopic features. Place dried specimens in labelled boxes, and keep them dry.

HOW TO IDENTIFY

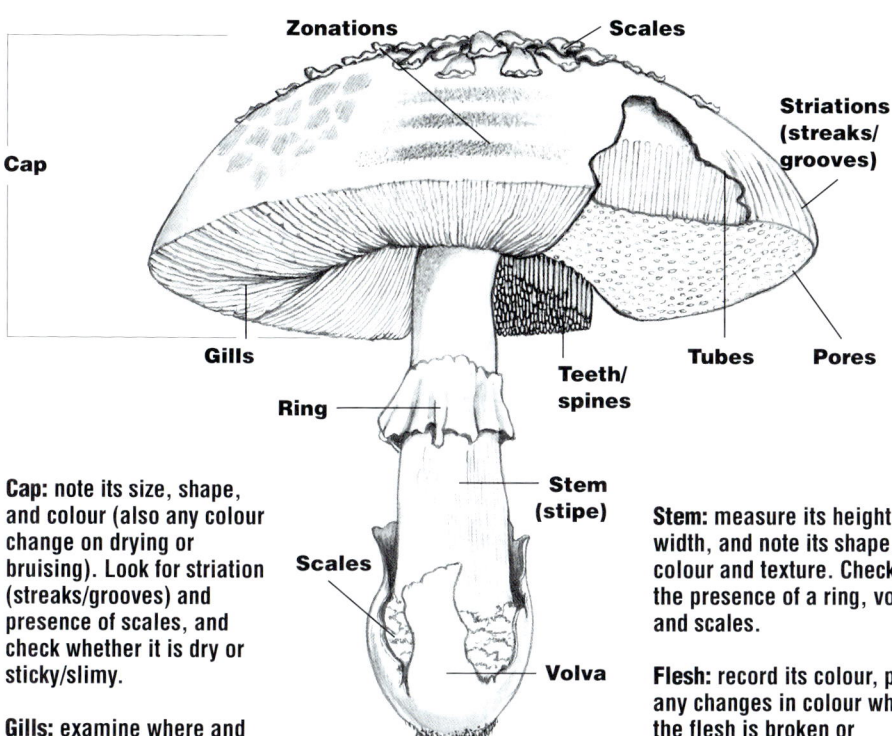

Diagram labels: Zonations, Scales, Striations (streaks/grooves), Cap, Gills, Tubes, Pores, Ring, Teeth/spines, Stem (stipe), Scales, Volva

Cap: note its size, shape, and colour (also any colour change on drying or bruising). Look for striation (streaks/grooves) and presence of scales, and check whether it is dry or sticky/slimy.

Gills: examine where and how they are attached to the cap/stem. Also notice their colour, shape, and whether they are crowded together or widely spaced.

Habitat: make a note of where the fungus is growing and what it is growing on.

Stem: measure its height and width, and note its shape, colour and texture. Check for the presence of a ring, volva and scales.

Flesh: record its colour, plus any changes in colour when the flesh is broken or bruised. Examine its texture, and check for the presence of 'milk'. If you find any, note its colour and whether it changes colour as it dries.

PROJECT

Preparing a spore deposit from a toadstool is quite easy and only takes a few hours. Cut off the stalk of a fresh specimen just below the cap, and place it on a sheet of paper. Use coloured paper if you think it will be a white deposit. Place a drop of water onto the cap so that it does not dry out, and cover it with a plastic box or similar container. This will help to keep the cap moist and prevent air movements from disrupting the deposit. After 6–8 hours, a deposit showing the gill arrangement will be formed.

EDIBLE OR POISONOUS?

Ten to eat:
Cep
Chanterelle
Dotted-stem bolete
Field mushroom
Giant puffball
Morel
Oyster mushroom
Parasol
Shaggy ink-cap
St George's mushroom
Wood blewit

Some to avoid:
Brown roll-rim
Cone-caps
Death cap
Destroying angel
Fairy-cakes
Fibre-caps
Fly agaric
Funnel-caps
Liberty cap
Panther cap
Pink-gills
Pixy-caps
Stinking parasol
Web-caps
Yellow stainer

Fungi have been a popular food for hundreds of years, even as far back as Roman times. A number of species, such as the truffle, cep, and of course the cultivated mushroom, are delicious and safe to eat. The great majority of fungi, however, are not edible. Most of these are simply too tough, or taste too bitter, but a few are dangerously poisonous. These fungi contain various toxins, and, while some only cause stomach upsets, others can be deadly. For this reason, never take risks – always check with an experienced adult before you eat any fungus you have found. Handle all species with care (wearing protective gloves if possible), and make sure that you wash your hands afterwards. Remember too that you should never eat an edible fungus that has been in the same collecting basket as a poisonous species.

The common mushroom (*Agaricus bisporus*) is the most widely grown fungus in Europe. It was first grown commercially in France in the 18th century, when the mushrooms were cultivated in cool, damp caves and old mines near Paris. Nowadays, *Agaricus bisporus* is grown in purpose-built chambers where the composition and moisture content of the culture soil are carefully regulated.

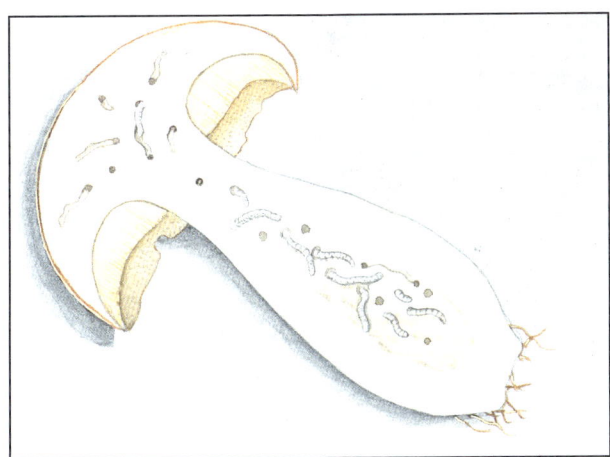

When collecting fungi for eating, it is very important that only fresh fruitbodies in good condition are chosen. Food poisoning from bad specimens of edible fungi is actually much more common than genuine poisoning from inedible species. Although many fungi are considered edible, allergic reactions or stomach upsets may occur in some people. Always try new fungi in small amounts to begin with.

Most of the deaths from fungus poisoning that occur in Europe are due to the death cap or one of its close relatives. Commonly found in oak woods in autumn, the death cap's olive-grey, streaky cap, and large ring and volva make it fairly easy to recognise. However, some of its relatives are entirely white. The species contains poisons which cause serious cell damage and, eventually, kidney and liver failure.

CONSERVATION

Like all living things, fungi need stable conditions in order to survive. If conditions within a particular habitat change or become unstable in some way, then the survival of the species adapted to live there will be threatened. Change may occur as a result of many different things – land development and various farming activities are most obvious, but fungi are also sensitive to changes in climate brought about, for example, by pollution in the upper atmosphere. Moisture in particular is essential to all fungi, and long periods of very hot, dry weather can drastically reduce their numbers.

Conservation – the protection of rare plants and animals so that they can continue to survive – has become a very important issue in the densely populated and polluted world of today. Like plants and animals, some species of fungi are also under threat – in many parts of Europe, their numbers, too, are dropping. This is especially true of fungi that grow in old, unmanaged grasslands and ancient woodlands, habitats that are all too often destroyed to make space for more farmland or for new buildings and roads. Even the good habitats that still remain are being spoilt, as chemicals from acid rain and from fertilisers find their way into the soil. Conservation of fungi is therefore of growing importance, and some species are now being included in many conservation schemes.

To help conservationists in their fight to preserve important areas of countryside and their wildlife, follow the country code when out on your foray:

- Always use gates and styles to cross walls, hedges or fences
- Make sure that all gates are closed properly
- Keep to the marked footpaths over farmland
- Keep dogs under control
- Leave no litter
- Guard against risk of fire
- Help to keep natural water sources clean

Many European fungi are, sadly, now considered to be endangered. Recently, studies have been made to work out which species are most under threat, and a list of ten (*below, far right*) has now been drawn up by the European Council for the Conservation of Fungi. They have been chosen from a range of habitats and represent various groups.

The list will eventually be submitted to the Council of Europe Convention on the Conservation of European Wildlife and Natural Habitats, to be held in Berne. If it is accepted, all ten species will become protected. However, many other fungi are also equally in danger and will need to be added to the list later.

- Poronia punctata
- Entoloma madidum
- Myriostoma coliforme (above)
- Torrendia pulchella
- Armillaria ectypa
- Aurantiporus croceus
- Boletus regius (left)
- Laricifomes officinalis
- Hericium clathroides
- Sarcosoma globosum

PROJECT

Visit a local grassland in the autumn, and look carefully for species of pink-gill and wax-cap, like this blackening wax-cap (*Hygrocybe conica*). Count how many different kinds you can find. You will probably only discover one or two of these rare fungi. But if you find several, the grassland may be an important site. The area may already be protected by law, but if not, it may well be worth passing the information on to your local conservation society.

FUNGI AND MAN

All the foods shown here can only be produced using various yeasts and moulds: bread and beer are fermented by yeasts, while blue cheese is ripened by the action of *Penicillium*.

Many kinds of fungi have a very important part to play in our lives. Some are medically important – the ringworm fungus, for example, causes an irritating skin disease, whilst some *Penicillium* moulds produce a powerful drug known as an antibiotic which helps to fight disease. Other kinds of fungi cause devastating crop diseases or destroy the timber of buildings. Yeasts are essential for the brewing of beer, and for making wine and many types of bread. Some fungi are also especially grown for food, the common mushroom being of particular importance in Europe.

Penicillin, an important antibiotic first discovered in 1928, is produced by *Penicillium* moulds. The drug kills harmful bacteria by attacking their protective cell walls and stopping them from developing properly.

PROJECT

You can observe the action of yeast for yourself by making bread. Find a suitable recipe in a cookery book, prepare the dough, and put it in a warm place (a). After a while, you'll see the dough begin to swell (b). What is happening is that the yeast is breaking down the sugar into alcohol and carbon dioxide gas. It is the gas bubbles which make the dough expand. When the bread is baked, the alcohol evaporates away, but the gas bubbles stay trapped in the bread (c).

a

b

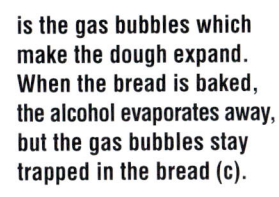

c

Dry rot fungus, *Serpula lacrymans*, is the most destructive of the fungi that grow in houses. It thrives on timber, making the wood so cracked and dry that it loses its strength. Dry rot spreads by cord-like structures and can grow through brickwork; once established, it is very difficult and extremely expensive to get rid of.

Ergots are hard, black, cylinder-shaped growths commonly seen in the flower heads of many grasses. They are produced by the fungus *Claviceps purpurea*, and are poisonous. Ergots were once very common in rye used for making bread. Many of the people who ate the poisonous bread developed serious nervous problems and some even died.

GARDENS AND PARKS

Gardens and parks, often with soil rich in nitrogen, provide many different habitats for fungi. The use of manures and fertilisers encourages the growth of species of *Coprinus*, *Conocybe*, *Agaricus* and numerous others. Parks may also include unfertilised grassy areas which, when old enough, support many fungi typical of natural grasslands. Old tree stumps provide a home for some wood-inhabiting species, while the wide variety of plant life means that parasitic fungi (see pp.8–9) and mycorrhizal fungi (see pp.8–9) also thrive.

Candle snuff fungus ▼
Found on old tree stumps, this fungus is named after the white powder that covers its upper branches in its early stage.

▼ **Fairy ring champignon**
A familiar sight in all grassy places, large numbers of this species often grow together, forming fairy rings.

▼ **Common white saddle**
A frequent parkland fungus, usually found along the edges of paths. Common white saddle may grow with other cup and saddle fungi.

◄ **Brown hay-cap**
A very common species of lawns and short grass; the dull brown, zoned caps appear from early summer.

Horse mushroom ▼
Often found in parkland, the white flesh of this large species smells of aniseed.

▼ **Orange peel fungus**
A colourful species which can be found at roadsides and along path edges in late autumn.

▼ **Wood blewit**
Common, especially in late autumn, the violet-coloured wood blewit may grow in large numbers, sometimes forming fairy rings on disturbed, nitrogen-rich soil.

Shaggy parasol ▼
Usually found near trees, the whitish flesh of shaggy parasol bruises pink when handled. The ring below the cap can be moved up and down on the stem.

Trumpet bird's-nest ▼
A fungus of disturbed soil and compost, especially in gardens. Each trumpet-shaped fruitbody contains several tiny 'eggs' which are splashed out by rain.

BOGS AND SWAMPS

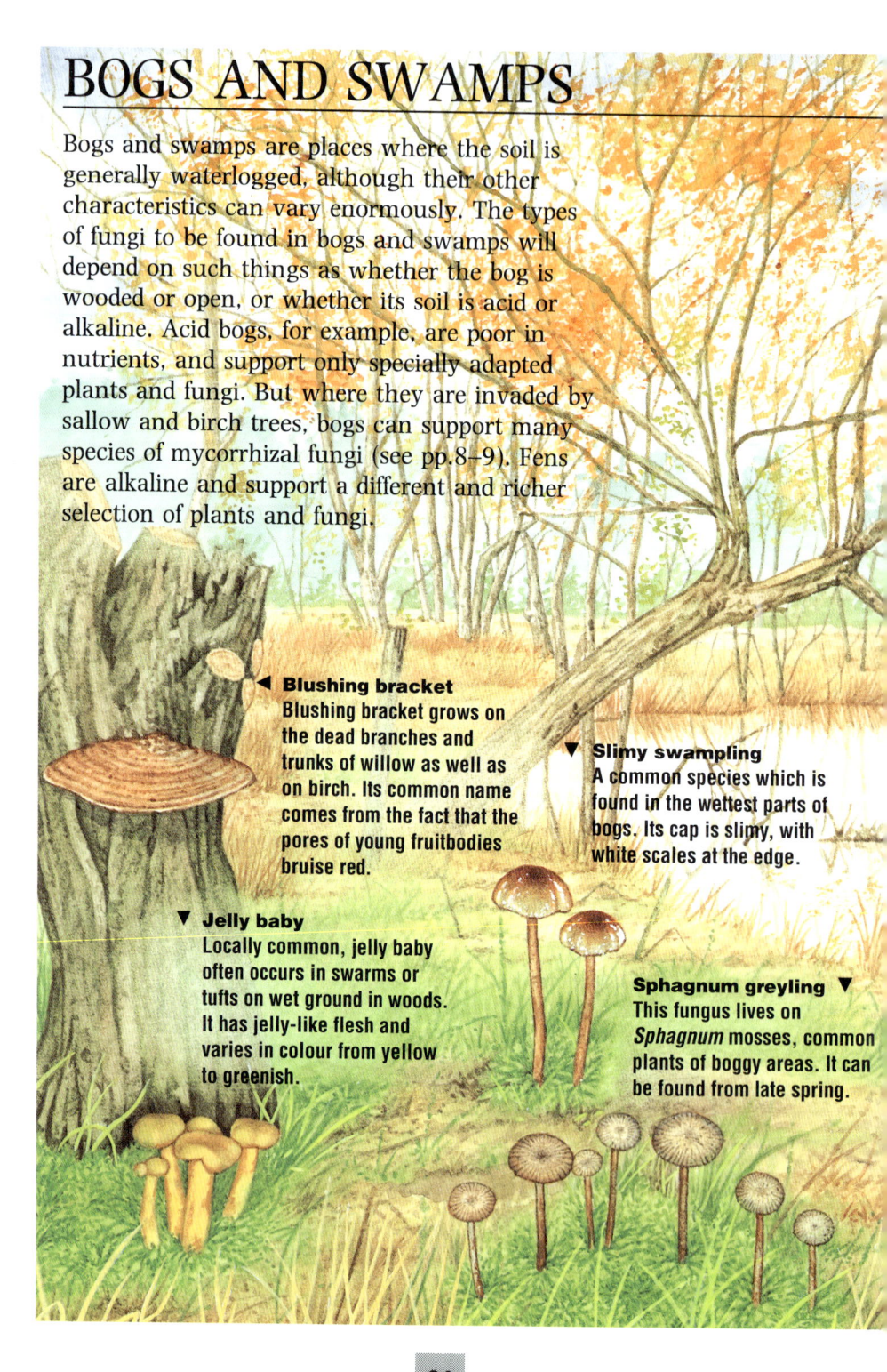

Bogs and swamps are places where the soil is generally waterlogged, although their other characteristics can vary enormously. The types of fungi to be found in bogs and swamps will depend on such things as whether the bog is wooded or open, or whether its soil is acid or alkaline. Acid bogs, for example, are poor in nutrients, and support only specially adapted plants and fungi. But where they are invaded by sallow and birch trees, bogs can support many species of mycorrhizal fungi (see pp.8–9). Fens are alkaline and support a different and richer selection of plants and fungi.

◀ **Blushing bracket**
Blushing bracket grows on the dead branches and trunks of willow as well as on birch. Its common name comes from the fact that the pores of young fruitbodies bruise red.

▼ **Jelly baby**
Locally common, jelly baby often occurs in swarms or tufts on wet ground in woods. It has jelly-like flesh and varies in colour from yellow to greenish.

▼ **Slimy swampling**
A common species which is found in the wettest parts of bogs. Its cap is slimy, with white scales at the edge.

Sphagnum greyling ▼
This fungus lives on *Sphagnum* mosses, common plants of boggy areas. It can be found from late spring.

24

Alder bracket ▼
This fungus grows in tiers on dead tree trunks, usually on alder, although it is sometimes found on birch and hazel.

Yellow swamp russule ▼
Bright yellow, sticky caps are characteristic of this fungus, which grows on damp ground, often under birch or amongst *Sphagnum* moss.

Bog pixy-cap ▼
One of the largest of the pixy-caps to be found in such habitats, this species can be recognised by its bright orange-yellow colour.

Orange bog web-cap ▼
This coppery-orange species grows at the edges of dried-up pools, usually under willow trees.

Alder milk-cap ▼
A small milk-cap, with a cap only 1–3cm across, this species is found from late spring under alder trees.

MEADOWS AND PASTURE

These include all grassland areas, most of which are now managed by farmers and at best only partly natural. Lawns and open grassland that have been fertilised support few plants other than common weeds such as dandelions, daisies and thistles. In these places, only fungi which can survive the high nitrogen levels in the soil are common. In untreated meadows, the plant life is much richer, and a wider range of fungi can be found. Earth-tongues, wax-caps, fairy-clubs and many pink-spored mushrooms all grow in unspoiled grassland.

Field mushroom ▼
One of the best known wild mushrooms, the gills of this species are pink when young. Its flesh turns slightly pinkish when bruised.

Scaly meadow puffball ▶
White and scaly at first, scaly meadow puffball breaks open when mature to release millions of brown, powdery spores.

Yellow cow-pat toadstool ▶
An attractive species with a lemon-yellow, slimy cap and thin flesh. Each cap quickly shrivels once it has matured.

PROJECT

Fields grazed by cattle or horses are good places to look for fungi adapted to nitrogen-rich soil. Visit one after damp weather in the autumn and collect specimens of the different fungi which are present. Make a list of those you find. Make a similar visit to an old, unfertilised meadow, such as one owned by a local Naturalist's Trust and, if necessary, get permission to collect the fungi. Compare the species lists that you obtain from the two sites.

Blackening wax-cap ▼
So-called because the flesh of this fungus blackens with age or when handled. It is common from late summer in many grassy habitats.

Meadow coral-fungus ▼
The branched, yellow fruitbodies of meadow coral-fungus can be found from late summer, usually in mossy grassland.

Parrot wax-cap ▼
This common, slime-covered species is usually green or yellow, although its colour can vary considerably.

Meadow wax-cap ▼
The distinctive, pale orange-brown caps of meadow wax-cap are frequently seen in meadows, although the species is sometimes found in other habitats.

Liberty cap ▲
Common in lawns and meadows and usually found in swarms, the olive-brown caps of this fungus have a raised point at their centre.

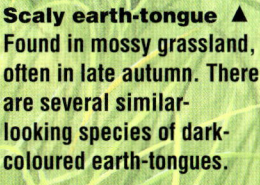

Scaly earth-tongue ▲
Found in mossy grassland, often in late autumn. There are several similar-looking species of dark-coloured earth-tongues.

27

BURNT GROUND

Burnt ground includes bonfire sites as well as larger-scale, accidental or deliberate burnings of woods or heaths. Intense burning makes the soil lifeless and more alkaline. On bonfire sites, mosses and algae are the first plants to appear, followed by various flowering plants. Some fungi are able to grow within a few months of burning. A succession of species follows, depending on the composition of the soil as the site develops. Different species are involved in this succession according to the habitat in which the fire occurs.

Bonfire chanterelle ▼
A distinctive but rather rare fungus which looks like a grey-coloured chanterelle. It does not usually appear until a year or so after the fire.

Purple bonfire cup ▼
The pale violet cups of this fungus are a common find on fire sites within a few months of burning.

Stalked bonfire cup ▼
This uncommon species is found on bare soil soon after burning, especially under conifer trees.

Common bonfire cup ▼
One of several small, orange cup fungi which grow in swarms on burnt sites. It appears soon after burning.

Shaggy bonfire ink-cap ▶
This common species can be recognised by the shaggy scales on its cap and stem. It also grows well on plaster.

▼ **Black bonnet-cap**
The stems of this species ooze white, milky drops when broken. It can be found in mossy places as well as on burnt ground.

Charcoal scale-head ▼
A common species which can appear on a burnt site fairly quickly and may continue to thrive for several years afterwards.

Bonfire navel-cap ▼
A distinctive, dark-coloured toadstool, with caps that often have a shallow 'pit' in the centre.

DUNG

Animal dung is a rich source of nutrients, and some fungi have become specially adapted to make use of it. Many species, covering all major groups, are involved, the greatest variety being found on the dung of plant-eating mammals such as cows, sheep and deer. The spores of many of these fungi are already present in the dung when it is produced, having been eaten by the animals as they grazed. Some fungi thrive on fresh dung, while others break down the undigested plant matter more slowly and appear later, creating a succession. The species present also vary according to the type of dung.

Dung liberty-cap ▼
Mainly found on old horse droppings, this is one of several types of fungi with purple-brown spores and a slimy cap.

Scurfy dung-cup ▼
One of many purple-spored cup fungi found on dung and elsewhere, this species has a scurfy outer surface.

Snow-white ink-cap ▼
This beautiful species, which is covered in a white mealy substance, is found mostly on horse dung.

Brown dung-cup ▼
Sometimes seen on old horse dung, brown dung-cup (*Peziza bovina*) is smaller and darker than the closely related bladder cup.

Little dung brush ▲
Very common, growing in swarms on many kinds of dung, the long, white hairs on the tiny cups of this species make them look like little brushes.

PROJECT

Rabbit droppings are very common in open woods and fields. Collect some fresh droppings and place them on damp tissue in a closed plastic box. Examine them daily, and keep them moist. Fungi will soon appear, growing from spores already present in the droppings. A succession of different species will appear over several weeks. Keep a note of the different kinds and how long they last.

Shiny hay-cap ▼
Pale, shiny caps and ringed stems characterise this fungus, which is a common sight on the dung of horses, sheep and cows.

▼ Fringed hay-cap
This species is easily recognized by its grey-brown cap, edged with white, tooth-like scales.

▼ Dung ink-cap
A tiny, reddish-brown coloured species which grows and disappears in a few hours, mainly on cow and horse dung.

▼ Shooting dung-fungus
This is one of several species of *Pilobolus*. All are tiny and have colourless stems with a black spore mass at the top.

▼ Dung orange-spot
The colourful, scurfy cups of dung orange-spot are commonly found in swarms on cow dung.

PINE WOODLAND

Natural pine woods occur on poor, sandy soils. As well as pine, they usually include other trees, such as rowan, and low shrubs, such as bilberry. There is often a thick carpet of needles on the ground, overgrown with various kinds of moss. These woods support a rich variety of fungi. In contrast, only a limited number of fungi can be found in pine plantations in areas where the tree is not native. Here, there are far fewer of the plants normally found growing in natural pine woods, and the needle litter, although thick, is not overgrown.

Plums-and-custard ▼
Named for its attractive purple and yellow colours, plums-and-custard is common on dead pine wood.

Violet conifer bracket ▼
A common bracket of dead conifer wood, this species can be recognised by its violet-coloured pores.

▲ **Jelly antler-fungus**
A colourful species with jelly-like flesh, unlike the fairy-club fungi which can look very similar.

◀ **False chanterelle**
Unlike the chanterelle itself, the false chanterelle has true gills, which are usually bright orange in colour.

PROJECT

Visit a pine wood in spring, and look for small, slender toadstools growing on the ground. These are species of *Strobilurus*, which are specially adapted to grow from buried pine cones. Carefully dig one up and find the cone from which it is growing. How deeply was it buried and how long is the stalk of the *Strobilurus* toadstool? Do the same with some others and compare the results.

Ear pick-fungus ▼
Named for its ear-shaped cap, which has spines on the underside, ear pick-fungus can be found all year-round, growing on buried pine cones.

Freckled flame-cap ▼
Common, sometimes in swarms on rotting branches on the woodland floor. The rusty spots on the cap and gills of this fungus develop with age.

Cauliflower fungus ▼
An unusual and distinctive fungus which can be found growing at the base of conifer trees.

Slippery Jack ▼
So-called because of its slimy cap, slippery Jack is found only with pine trees.

◀ **Chanterelle**
Chanterelle can be found under deciduous trees such as oak and beech as well as in pine woods. It has thick, vein-like ridges underneath its cap instead of gills.

SPRUCE-LARCH WOODLAND

Spruce woodland is found in parts of continental Europe but does not occur naturally in Britain. Larch can be found growing on the mountains of central and southeast Europe, but is also frequently planted elsewhere. The trees are often planted very close together, so other plant life is usually limited, and the ground is covered with a thick needle litter. Spruce woods support many species of mycorrhizal fungi (see pp.8–9), but fewer such species occur with larch.

Larch bolete ▼
Frequent wherever larch trees grow, this species can be identified by its slimy yellow or orange cap and the whitish ring on its stem.

Scaly wood mushroom ▼
Usually found in thick needle litter, this species has white flesh which turns red when damaged or broken.

Orange-zoned bracket ▼
Orange-zoned bracket is found on deciduous trees as well as on conifers. It is very rare in Britain, although common elsewhere.

Silky-grey knight-cap ▶
A streaky grey cap is characteristic of this fungus, which is fairly common in natural forest, although less so in plantations.

Spotted tough-shank ▶
This very common species is entirely white at first, later becoming flecked with red-brown spots.

Bitter bracket ▼
Bitter bracket is common on various conifers. Its flesh is white and spongy.

Spruce milk-cap ▼
Common in young spruce plantations. The 'milk' that spruce milk-cap oozes when damaged slowly turns from orange to green.

Slender truffle-club ▼
A common species which only grows on Hart's truffle. Yellow strands at its base lead down to the deeply buried truffle.

Ochre-green coral-fungus ▶
Fairly common amongst needle litter, this green-tinged species often forms fairy rings.

Hart's truffle ▶
This fungus grows below the ground, sometimes several centimetres down in the soil. Its spores are powdery black when mature.

DECIDUOUS WOODLAND 1

Beech trees are characteristic of deciduous woods found on well-drained, rich or chalky soil. Few other woody plants can grow under beech trees, since their leaves block out most of the light – but herbs, such as wood anemone, which flower in the spring before the trees come into leaf, are common. Many kinds of mycorrhizal fungi (see pp.8–9) occur with beech, while other species grow on the fallen, rotting wood. Forests of ash are more common on damper chalky soil. Ash trees grow with a wide variety of other plants and they do not support any mycorrhizal fungi at all. Some species of *Lepiota* are common in ash forests, and many other fungi grow on the dead wood.

Artist's fungus ▼
This common bracket is found on the dead and dying trunks of beech and other trees. It is often infested with midges, which live in tiny, swollen galls on its underside, but these are very rare in Britain.

Dotted-stem bolete ▼
Often found with beech, the flesh of this species turns dark blue when cut.

Lilac bonnet-cap ▼
One of the few lilac-coloured toadstools, this fungus grows in leaf litter. Its flesh smells of radishes.

Beech jelly-disc ▼
An attractive pinkish cup fungus, found in clusters on the bark of recently fallen trunks and branches.

▼ **The charcoal burner**
A common member of the *Russula* genus, the gills of this mushroom are more flexible than those of its close relatives.

◄ **Porcelain fungus**
The easily identified, almost see-through, fruitbodies of this species often grow in tufts, perched high on dead branches of beech.

Cramp balls ▼
Found mainly on ash, the fruitbodies of this fungus look as if they have been burnt – hence its other common name, 'King Alfred's cakes'.

If you cut open some fruitbodies of cramp balls (*Daldinia concentrica*), you'll see that the flesh inside has alternate light and dark zones, like the rings in a tree stump. These zones are thought to be a special adaptation of the fungus to help conserve water in case of dry periods.

Stinking parasol ▼
Very common, occurring in small clusters amongst leaf litter and along the edges of paths.

Horn-of-plenty ▼
Usually clustered in leaf litter, horn-of-plenty is often very difficult to find due to its dark grey colour.

Hedgehog puffball ▼
So-called because of its long spines, which are best seen when the fungus is young and fresh.

DECIDUOUS WOODLAND 2

Deciduous woodland found on acid soil, which is poor in nutrients, can vary enormously. Oak and birch are common trees of this soil type, and there is often a well-developed shrub layer including species such as alder buckthorn and bilberry. Ferns and mosses are common, as are herbs such as wood sage and wood-sorrel. The leaf litter breaks down slowly and the soil is humus-rich. Such conditions support many mycorrhizal fungi (see pp.8–9). Decaying wood also provides an important habitat for many species of fungi.

Oak bonnet-cap ▼
Found on logs and stumps of oak and sweet chestnut, oak bonnet-cap can be identified by its reddish-yellow stem base and rancid, spicy smell.

◄ **Beefsteak fungus**
The red, juicy flesh of this species looks like ox tongue. It grows on old oak and sweet chestnut, often on the living trees.

▼ **Purple-black russule**
The purplish-red cap of this species has a darker centre. It is frequently seen growing under oak trees.

Common earthball ▼
Most often seen in damp places in woods, common earthball is sometimes found with the parasitic bolete (*Boletus parasiticus*) growing on it.

▲ **Spindle shank**
This red-brown fungus, with its strange, spindle-shaped stem, grows in tufts on the roots of oak and sometimes other trees.

Birch polypore ▼
A very common bracket fungus which is always found on dead birch. It often causes the top of the tree to break off.

Orange birch bolete ▼
A common and distinctive species, the stem of this orange-capped fungus is typically dotted with brown or black scales.

Brown roll-rim ▼
A very common species, almost always found with birch. The rolled edges of the brownish-coloured cap are distinctly furry.

Fly agaric ▲
This familiar, 'fairy-tale' toadstool is most often found growing with birch, although it also occurs with conifers.

DUNES AND HEATHLAND

Dunes, usually found along the coast, are created by the wind as it blows around and piles up the fine sand. Dunes become much more fixed and firm where plants, such as marram grass, grow on them, binding the sand grains together with their roots. Heathlands are found on poor, acid soils in parts of northern Europe. Typical heathland plants include heathers, gorse and crowberry, and lichens are also common. Both dunes and heathland support a variety of specially adapted fungi.

Marram bonnet-cap ▼
This species grows singly or in tufts at the base of marram grass in outer dunes. It fruits until the beginning of winter.

Marram brittle-head ▶
The commonest white dune species, always growing with marram grass, this mushroom helps to bind the sand at the base of its stem.

Parasol mushroom ▼
Common in white dunes and inner dunes as well as in other habitats, this is one of the largest European mushrooms.

◀ Common brown fibre-cap
Found in inner dunes, growing with creeping willow, often around pools. This species is also found on sandy soil in other habitats.

PROJECT

Dunes have two main zones; outer, unstable white dunes and inner, stable dunes, with creeping willow growing on them. Compare the fungi that you find in these two zones. Walk about 250m along the outer dunes and back along the inner ones. Collect or note the fungi found in each zone. Estimate how many species and fruitbodies are only found in one zone or the other, and how many are common to both zones.

Dune cup ▼
A fairly common white dune species, dune cup grows partly buried in sand. It has a 'false' stem, formed of bound sand grains.

Dune stinkhorn ▶
Dune stinkhorn (*Phallus hadriani*) grows with marram grass in outer dunes. Unlike common stinkhorn, the 'egg' from which the fruitbody develops is pink, not white.

Dune wax-cap ▼
A very attractive fungus which is mainly found in inner dunes. Other species of wax-caps may also occur in this habitat.

Dune earth-tongue ▼
A fungus of sandy soil, often growing with crowberry. The black fruitbodies look like lumps of oil or tar.

Heath navel-cap ▼
Frequent on heathland, this navel-cap can be found growing amongst mosses and lichens.

Horse-hair fungus ▼
This fungus grows on the dead stems of ling on heathland. It is also often seen in conifer woods.

Dwarf earth-star ▼
This fungus grows only in dunes which contain a lot of lime in their sandy soil.

Heath fairy-club ▲
This yellow-stemmed species usually grows with crowberry on heathland. It is often found alongside dune earth-tongue.

CUP FUNGI 1

COMMON WHITE SADDLE
Helvella crispa
H 6–15cm, CW 3–6cm, SW 2–3cm. Cream or yellowish saddle-shaped cap and tall, white, deeply furrowed stem. Common. Fr 7–11; Wd, P; S.

GENERAL FEATURES

The fungi shown here and on the following six pages are popularly known as cup fungi. Many of them have cup- or saucer-shaped fruitbodies, and their spores are produced in tiny, sac-like structures called asci (see pp.4–5). The asci of the species on this and the next four pages are thin-walled, opening at the top by a lid which allows the spores to be shot out. The cup fungi shown here are amongst the largest and most easily recognised. Most of them are found in the autumn months, except the morels and ribbed saddle which appear in the spring.

Morels are amongst the best edible fungi, and are much sought after throughout Europe and North America. They must, however, be well cooked before being eaten. However, the false morels (*Gyromitra*), which have a brain-like cap (shown here), can cause severe poisoning.

HABITATS

These cup fungi can be found on soil, or amongst decaying leaves, in many different habitats. Most occur in woods, but orange peel fungus often grows on paths, or even between paving stones in towns. Morels can appear in unusual places, such as gardens and rubbish tips, but are most often found on alkaline soil in woods and dunes.

LEMON PEEL FUNGUS
Otidea onotica
H 5–8cm, W 2–4cm. Rabbit ear-shaped fruitbody, yellowish with pink tinges; usually found in clusters. One of several similar species, ranging from yellow to dark brown in colour.
Fr 9–11; Wd; S.

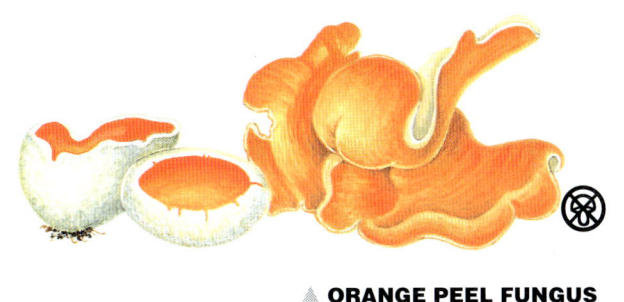

ORANGE PEEL FUNGUS
Aleuria aurantia
H 5–15mm, W 2–19cm. Cup-shaped, stalkless fruitbody, bright orange inside, paler underneath. Common.
Fr 8–11; PE, P, W; S.

ELASTIC SADDLE
Helvella elastica
H 5–10cm, CW 2–4cm, SW 5–10mm. Saddle-shaped, grey-brown cap, paler underneath. Stem whitish, hollow. Fairly common.
Fr 8–11; Wd, PE, P; S.

RIBBED SADDLE
Helvella acetabula
H 3–8cm, W 2–6cm. Goblet-shaped with blunt ribs on outside; stem short and ribbed. Pale brown in colour, with paler stem; downy at the rim. Frequent on alkaline soil. Fr 5–6; Wd, H, P; S.

COMMON MOREL
Morchella esculenta
H 7–25cm, CW 4–10cm, SW 2–6cm. Yellow or brown, honeycomb-like cap and whitish, flaky stem. Uncommon, on alkaline soil.
Fr 4–6; P, W, Wd, PE; S.

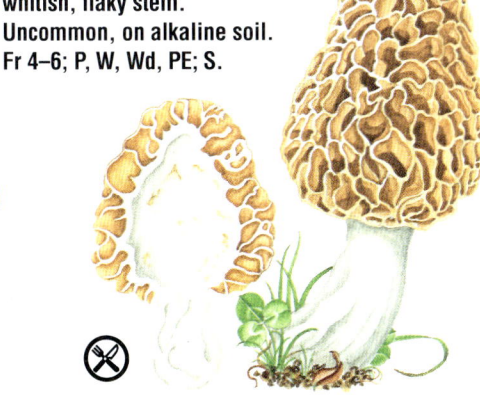

CUP FUNGI 2

GENERAL FEATURES

The fungi shown here have simple, cup-shaped fruitbodies. Most belong to the large genus *Peziza*, members of which are found all over the world. Species of *Peziza* are often difficult to tell apart – colour and habitat are important clues, but sometimes they can only be correctly identified by examination under a microscope. A few have yellow or blue juice. The bonfire cup belongs to a different family.

HABITATS

Species of *Peziza* can be found in a variety of habitats. Many occur on soil, but some are specialists, being found on dung, wood or plaster. *Peziza ammophila* can only be found in dunes, whilst several other species occur on rotten wood, the commonest of these being *Peziza micropus* and the larger *Peziza arvernensis*. Bonfire sites are also rich in cup fungi, including the stalked bonfire cup.

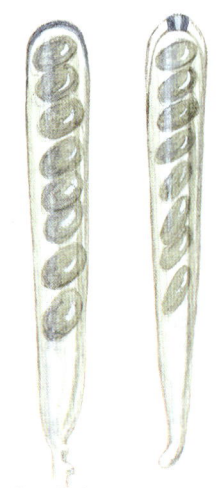

The tips of the asci of all members of the genus *Peziza* stain blue when placed in iodine solution, unlike the asci of other similar cup fungi. This is one way that fungi experts (mycologists) recognise different groups of species.

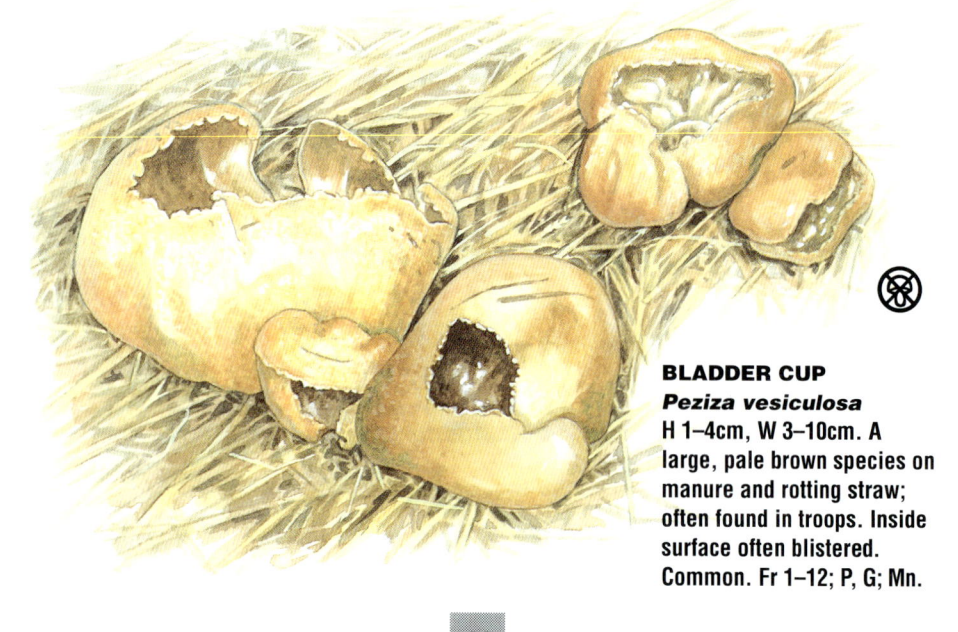

BLADDER CUP
Peziza vesiculosa
H 1–4cm, W 3–10cm. A large, pale brown species on manure and rotting straw; often found in troops. Inside surface often blistered. Common. Fr 1–12; P, G; Mn.

DUNE CUP
Peziza ammophila
H 3–5cm including stem, W 2–4cm. Yellowish brown, deeply cup-shaped. Always buried in sand, binding sand grains below to form a false stem. Fairly common, with marram grass. Fr 9–11; D.

YELLOW-MILK CUP
Peziza succosa
H 1cm, W 1.5–6cm. Pale brown, with easily broken flesh and juice which turns yellow. Frequent. Fr 7–11; CWd, DWd; S.

PURPLE BONFIRE CUP
Peziza praetervisa
H 5–10mm, W 1–5cm. Saucer-shaped fruitbody with brittle flesh, sometimes clustered. Inner surface brown-purple, paler underneath. Frequent. Fr 3–11: B.

PROJECT

Cup fungi often release their spores in clouds by shooting out a large number at the same time. To see this happen, blow across a mature fruitbody or place it in a closed container for a few hours. The effect should be easy to see when the container is opened.

STALKED BONFIRE CUP
Geopyxis carbonaria
H 2–3cm, W 1–2cm. Goblet-shaped with short stem – cap edge finely toothed. Inside pinkish-brown, outside paler. Occasional. Fr 8–10; B.

45

CUP FUNGI 3

GENERAL FEATURES
A variety of other larger cup fungi are shown here. Many species have hairs of various kinds, as can be clearly seen in the eye-lash fungus. Some have bright-coloured fruitbodies, particularly orange or red. A few have coloured spores, notably the tiny *Ascobolus* species in which the spores are violet.

HABITATS
Damp or wet, often mossy, ground is an ideal habitat for many cup fungi. The eye-lash fungus is common on rotten wood and soil in these places. Some, such as species of *Octospora*, grow directly on mosses. Scarlet elf-cup can be found in damp, mossy ground in limey areas. This beautiful fungus grows on rotten twigs and small branches and occurs in late winter and early spring. Dung is also an important habitat, different species occurring on the dung of different animals.

The spores of larger cup fungi are often oval in shape, although some are rounded. Many are colourless, but a few are brown or purple. The spore surface may be smooth, but in many species it is ornamented with warts or ridges.

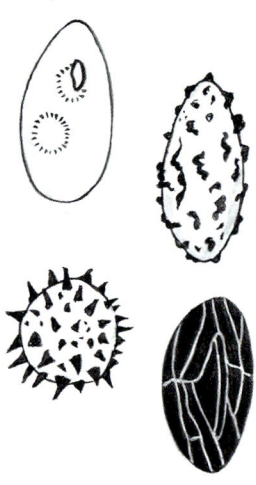

SCARLET ELF-CUP
Sarcoscypha coccinea
H 1.5–4cm, W 1–5cm. Cup scarlet red on the inside, paler and downy on the outside. Uncommon.
Fr 12–4; DWd; W.

EYE-LASH FUNGUS
Scutellinia scutellata
H 2–3mm, W 5mm–1cm. Disc-shaped, bright orange-red with a fringe of dark brown hairs. Often found in swarms in damp places. Common. Fr 5–11; DWd, H; W, S.

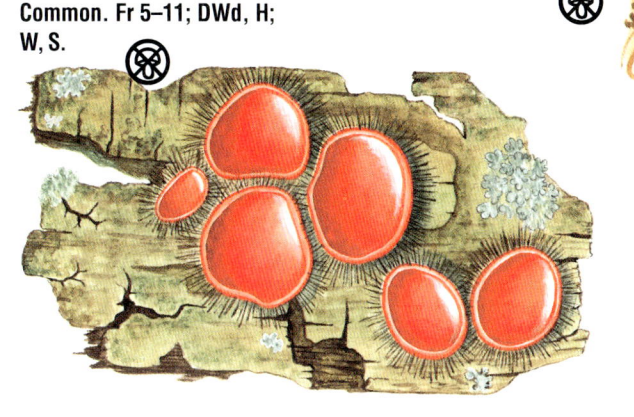

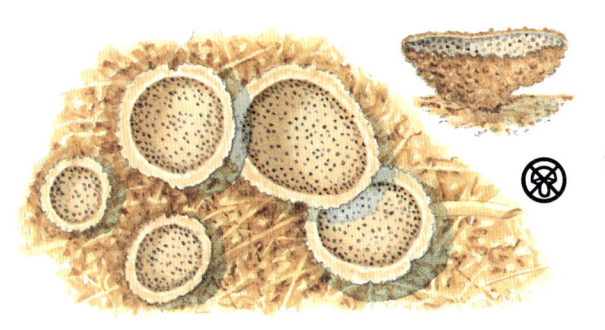

DUNG ORANGE-SPOT
Coprobia granulata
H 0.5mm, W 1–2mm. Tiny, yellow-orange discs which have a surface covered in little grains. This species is very common, growing in swarms on cow dung. It is easy to find and easy to recognise. Fr 1–12; Dg (cow pastures).

COMMON BONFIRE CUP
Anthracobia maurilabra
H 0.5–1mm, W 1–5mm. Disc-shaped when mature. Pale orange, streaked on the outside with bunches of dark brown hairs. In swarms on bonfire sites. Common. Fr 6–10; B.

SCURFY DUNG-CUP
Ascobolus furfuraceus
H 0.5–1mm, W 1–5mm. Flattened and disc-shaped when mature. Yellow-brown in colour, with projecting, purplish asci. Common. Fr 1–12; Dg, L.

CUP FUNGI 4

JELLY BABY
Leotia lubrica
H 3–6cm, CW 5–10mm, SW 3–7mm. Greenish-yellow, rounded cap; yellow stem. Jelly-like flesh. Common. Fr 8–11; DWd, M; S.

GENERAL FEATURES

The asci (see pp.4–5) of all the fungi shown here are thickened at the tip, with a pore through which the spores are forced out. Most of this group are tiny, many of them less than 1mm across. However, they are extremely variable in size, form and texture. Although many are cup- or disc-shaped, others are club-shaped or tongue-like in form. A few of the larger ones have a jelly-like flesh.

HABITATS

These fungi occur in a wide range of habitats, although most are found on rotten stems and leaves. They are rarely found on dung, and only a few, such as those of the earth-tongue family, grow on soil. A few are parasites, causing destructive plant diseases.

Apples are often attacked by various fungi. One of the commonest is *Monilinia fructigena*, which causes brown rot. It produces small, woolly, pale brown spots on brown, rotting patches and can be very destructive to crops and stored fruit.

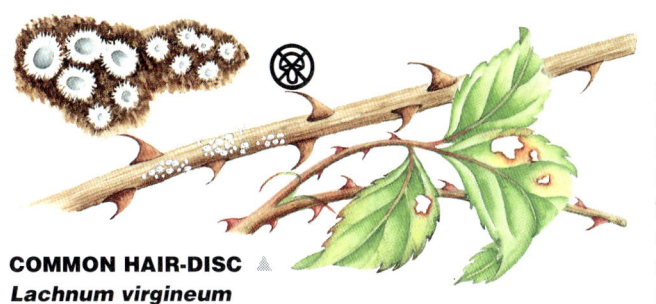

COMMON HAIR-DISC
Lachnum virgineum
H 1–2mm, W 0.5–1mm. A white fungus, hairy on the outer surface. Very common, in swarms. Fr 1–12; Wd, H, P, Hl; L.

DUNE EARTH-TONGUE
Geoglossum arenarium
H 1–5cm, W 1–2cm. Blackish 'tongues', often joined together in clusters, binding sand into a clump. Grows with crowberry. Local. Fr 10–4; D, Hl; S.

SCALY EARTH-TONGUE
Geoglossum fallax
H 3–6cm, W 3–6mm. Blackish-brown all over, stem dry and scaly. Uncommon. Fr 8–11; Md, DWd; S.

BEECH JELLY-DISC
Neobulgaria pura
H 5–10mm, W 1–3cm. An attractive, pinkish fungus, with jelly-like flesh. Frequent, often found in clusters on beech. Fr 7–11; DWd; W.

BOG BEACON
Mitrula paludosa
H 2–6cm, W 3–8mm. Bright yellow or orange head and white stem. Grows on rotten leaves in boggy places. Frequent. Fr 4–6; M, DWd; L.

TRUFFLES AND FLASK FUNGI

CANDLE SNUFF FUNGUS
Xylaria hypoxylon
H 2–7cm, W 3–10mm.
Upright, with black, hairy stem; forked and white above when young. Very common. Fr 1–12; Wd, P; W.

GENERAL FEATURES

The fungi shown here are all fungi that have asci, although the form of their fruitbodies varies considerably. Truffles mature below ground, releasing their spores as the fruitbody decays. Flask fungi produce their spores in flask-shaped structures which may be found both singly or in groups.

HABITATS

Truffles grow with living trees and occur where the host tree thrives. Some prefer alkaline soils, others need acidic conditions. Flask fungi can be found in almost any habitat, even occurring on living or dead insects or as parasites on truffles. The majority occur on plants.

True truffles – like this summer truffle (*Tuber aestivum*) – are the most expensive of all edible fungi. Truffling is an ancient tradition in Europe. Pigs or dogs are trained to detect the strong-smelling, mature truffles which grow underground.

◀ **SLENDER TRUFFLE-CLUB**
Cordyceps ophioglossoides
H 5–10cm, W 5–10mm. Club-shaped, head yellow-green at first, then olive-black. Parasitic on Hart's truffle. Occasional. Fr 7–11; Wd.

RED WOOD-WART ▶
Hypoxylon fragiforme
H 3–10mm, W 3–10mm. Roundish, red-brown fruitbody with rough surface and black, coal-like flesh. Very common, on beech. Fr 1–12; DWd; W.

▲ **CRAMP BALLS**
Daldinia concentrica
H 1–4cm, W 2–10cm. Brown at first, then black and shiny. Flesh with dark and light concentric zones. Frequent. Fr 1–12; DWd, P; W.

◀ **HART'S TRUFFLE**
Elaphomyces granulatus
H 2–4cm, W 2–4cm. Roundish, with yellowish-brown, warted surface. Fairly common, growing several centimetres underground. Fr 3–10; CWd, DWd; S.

HOW TO FIND

There are many tiny species of flask fungi to be found on rotten leaves, stems and branches of all kinds. An example is *Leptosphaeria acuta*, (shown here), which is common and easily found on last year's stems of nettle. Some of the larger and more conspicuous flask fungi can be found on piles of logs or on old stumps.

JELLY FUNGI

YELLOW BRAIN FUNGUS
Tremella mesenterica
W 1–10cm. Yellow or orange, lobed and folded. Hard and horny when dry. Common.
Fr 1–12; P, H, Hl, Wd; W.

GENERAL FEATURES

Almost all of these fungi have jelly-like fruitbodies. They have no protection against drying out, but they do recover easily when damp conditions return. They all produce their spores on structures called basidia (see p.5), and the structure of the basidia helps to tell the different groups apart. The basidia in jelly fungi are of three different kinds and are unlike those of toadstools and brackets. These fungi range from simple, spot-like growths to large, stalked or toothed structures.

HABITATS

Most of these species are only found on rotten wood, including timber in buildings such as damp window frames. Commonly, individual species are restricted to one, or a few, host trees. Some groups of jelly fungi include species which produce their fruitbodies on, or even inside, other fungi.

The popular name of *Auricularia auricula-judae* – 'Jew's Ear' – may have come from 'Judas' Ear'. This refers to a common belief that Judas hanged himself from an elder tree, the common host of this fungus.

COMMON JELLY SPOT
Dacrymyces stillatus
H 0.5–2mm, W 1–5mm.
Orange-yellow at first,
turning darker with age. In
swarms on rotten wood. Very
common. Fr 1–12; W.

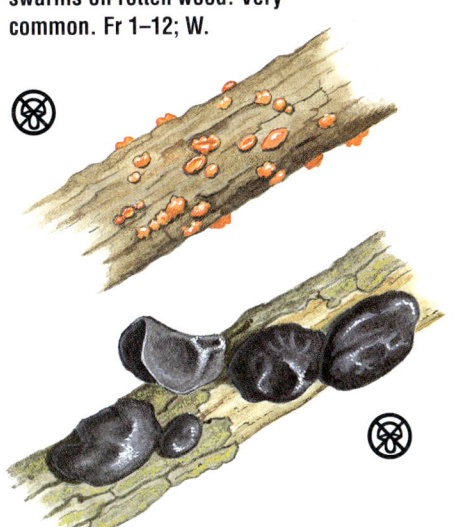

BLACK BRAIN FUNGUS
Exidia glandulosa
H 2–10mm, W 2–10 ×
2–5cm. Blackish, with
surface roughened by small
warts. Common. Fr 1–12;
DWd, P; W.

JEW'S EAR
Auricularia auricula-judae
H 1–3cm, W 2–10cm. Ear-
shaped; upper surface brown,
hairy, underside grey-brown.
Common, especially on elder.
Fr 1–12; P, Wd, H; W.

PROJECT

Find one of the species illustrated (*Tremella mesenterica* is shown below). Let the specimen dry out on a windowsill, then place it in water. Like all jelly fungi but few others, it will swell and regain its normal size. Next, try to get a spore deposit from the revived specimen by laying it on a sheet of coloured paper, enclosed in a container so that it does not dry out. Most jelly fungi have white spores.

Fresh   **Dried**

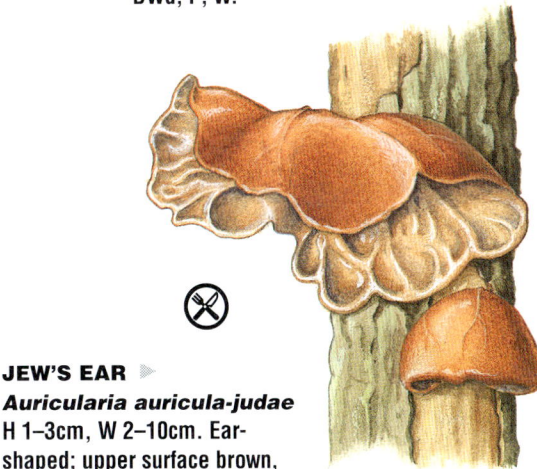

JELLY ANTLER-FUNGUS
Calocera viscosa
H 2–10cm, SW 2–4mm.
Bright yellow to orange;
upright, branched, with
rubbery flesh. Common, on
conifers. Fr 7–11; CWd, P; W.

STOMACH FUNGI 1

GENERAL FEATURES

All of these fungi are basidiomycetes (see pp.4–5) that develop their spores inside closed fruitbodies. This group includes species from various families such as stinkhorns, puffballs, earth-stars and bird's-nest fungi. They all have different methods of spreading their spores. Puffballs, for example, release their spores either through a pore or by irregular breakdown of the wall. In earth-stars, the outer wall breaks up into rays which turn back to expose and raise the inner, spore-containing body.

HABITATS

These species all grow on soil in a variety of habitats. Several can be found on open grassland, lawns and inner dunes, whilst others, including many of the true puffballs, are woodland fungi.

The giant puffball is one of the largest known fungi. A diameter of over 150cm has been claimed for this species, although an average fruitbody is the size of a football. One fruitbody produces about 7,000,000,000,000 spores.

GIANT PUFFBALL
Langermannia gigantea
H 10–25cm, W 20–50cm. Roundish fruitbody; white at first, becoming yellowish and finally brown. Surface leathery, but papery when old. Spore mass olive brown. Occasional, sometimes in fairy rings. Fr 7–10; P, G, H, Wd; S.

SCALY MEADOW PUFFBALL
Calvatia utriformis
H 5–20cm, W 5–15cm. White at first, with obvious scales on upper part – later brownish. Stem-like base; spore mass brown. Frequent.
Fr 5–11; Md, Hl, P, D; S.

BLACK BOVISTA
Bovista nigrescens
H 2–4cm, W 3–5cm. White at first, outer layer flaking off to expose brownish inner wall. Spore mass brown. Frequent.
Fr 7–11; Md, G, P; S.

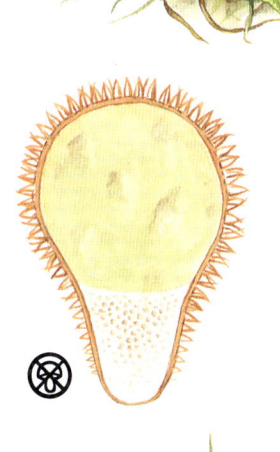

HEDGEHOG PUFFBALL
Lycoperdon echinatum
H 2–6cm, W 2–5cm. Brown when ripe, with long spines. When the spines fall off, they leave a distinctive 'net' pattern behind. Spore mass purple-brown. Uncommon, in woods on alkaline soil.
Fr 7–11; DWd; S.

DWARF EARTH-STAR
Geastrum nanum
H 1.5–2.5cm, W 2–3cm. Five to eight pointed rays; inner part has a short stem, and a cone-shaped, grooved 'mouth'. Uncommon.
Fr 8–11; D; S.

STOMACH FUNGI 2

COMMON STINKHORN
Phallus impudicus
H 12–20cm, CW 2.5–3.5cm, SW 2–3cm. Egg white, jelly-like, with white strands at base. Stem whitish, hollow and polystyrene-like. Dark olive spore mass. Common. Fr 6–10; Wd, P, H; S, W.

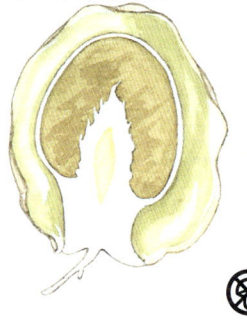

GENERAL FEATURES

Three groups of stomach fungi are shown here. Earthballs are similar to puffballs, but they have black spores and fruitbodies with only a single, although often thick and scaly, wall. Bird's-nest fungi are a unique group, having small, egg-like bodies which contain spores. In typical members of the group, the eggs lie within a 'nest'-like structure. Stinkhorns are quite different, having jelly-like 'eggs' from which the stem and spore-bearing part are produced. They can expand rapidly, using the water contained in the jelly. The spore mass is slimy and smells unpleasant.

Flies and other insects are attracted to the stinking, slimy spore mass of common stinkhorn. When they fly off after feeding, they carry away spores stuck on to their bodies. This is the way in which the stinkhorn spreads to new locations.

HABITATS

Most species occur on soil, often in woodland. Some are specialised in habitat, an example being the dune stinkhorn. Bird's-nest fungi often occur on rotten vegetation or even on dung. Earthballs are mycorrhizal (see pp.8–9).

COMMON EARTHBALL
Scleroderma citrinum
H 3–7cm, W 5–15cm.
Roundish fruitbody with
white strands at base. Wall
thick and scaly. Spore mass
purple-black. Smell metallic.
Common. Fr 7–11; DWd,
Hl, P; S.

SHOOTING STAR
Sphaerobolus stellatus
H 1–2mm, W 1–2mm. Round
fruitbody splits into rays,
shooting spore-body several
metres. Common. Fr 6–11;
W, P, Wd, Md, G, D; L, Dg.

TRUMPET BIRD'S-NEST
Cyathus olla
H 8–15mm, W 8–12mm.
Trumpet-shaped, with hairy
outer surface and smooth,
grey, inner surface. Eggs
pale grey. Common. Fr 6–11;
P, W, D; L.

DOG STINKHORN
Mutinus caninus
H 10–12cm, W 1–1.5cm. Egg
elongated; stem slender,
whitish, hollow. Cap orange,
with olive-brown spore
mass. Frequent. Fr 7–10;
DWd; S.

PROJECT

Carefully collect some stinkhorn eggs
from your local woods. Back at home,
place them in loose soil in a flower pot
or other suitable container. Keep them
moist and watch as they expand and
develop. Remember that they have a
strong, unpleasant smell, so store them
outside if possible!

BRACKET FUNGI 1

ARTIST'S FUNGUS
Ganoderma applanatum
H 3–9cm at base, W 15–60 × 8–25cm. Upper surface with brown crust and white edge. Flesh red brown with white patches. Common. Perennial (lives on from year to year). DWd, P; W.

GENERAL FEATURES

The fungi shown here are among the largest of the bracket fungi. They all have bracket- or shelf-like fruitbodies, with the spores produced in tubes on the underside of the bracket. They vary greatly in form, and may or may not have a stem. The upperside of the bracket may be smooth or hairy, and is sometimes grooved or zoned. The species also vary greatly in texture – they may be hard or soft, tough or cheese-like.

HABITATS

Bracket fungi commonly grow on trees, many of them causing a serious rot which eventually kills the tree. Others occur only on dead wood, some of them on the timber of buildings where they also rot the wood, sometimes causing costly damage. Three of the species on these two pages are perennial – they live on from year to year, growing a new layer of tubes each season.

Ganoderma applanatum, like some of its relatives, has a whitish, spore-producing surface which bruises brown at the slightest touch. It is easy to write or draw on this surface, and the species is popularly known as 'artist's fungus' for this reason.

BEECH BRACKET
Pseudotrametes gibbosa
H 2–5cm, W 6–20 × 4–15cm. Upper surface zoned, whitish, often green with algae. Spore-producing tubes long and whitish. Common, especially on beech. Fr 1–12; DWd; W.

ORANGE-ZONED BRACKET
Fomitopsis pinicola
H 5–15cm, W 5–25 × 5–12cm. Hoof-shaped; upper surface zoned, dark at the base, orange near the white edge. Common in Central Europe, rare in Britain. Perennial (lives on from year to year). Wd; W.

SHINY BRACKET
Ganoderma lucidum
H 1–3cm, W 10–25 × 6–15cm. Stem up to 25cm long. Distinctive, red-brown, shiny crust. Occasional. Fr 6–11; CWd, DWd, P; W.

TINDER FUNGUS
Fomes fomentarius
H 10–25cm, W 10–30 × 5–20cm. Hoof-shaped, with hard, smooth, greyish surface. Locally common. Perennial (lives on from year to year), especially on beech and birch. DWd, P; W.

59

BRACKET FUNGI 2

GENERAL FEATURES

The brackets shown here are not all closely related, but each one has annual fruitbodies, which means that they complete their life cycle in one year. Species of *Trametes*, *Daedaleopsis* and *Trichaptum* are thin, tough and leathery, while *Piptoporus* has thick, firm flesh. Also shown is one representative of the large group *Tyromyces*, with soft, cheese-like flesh.

HABITATS

The birch polypore occurs only on birch, normally fruiting when the tree is dead but still upright. In contrast, the blushing bracket grows on many hosts, although it is most common on willow. The violet conifer bracket grows on most conifers but never on deciduous trees. Bitter bracket grows mainly on dead conifers, whilst the many-zoned polypore is found only on broad-leaved trees.

Razor strop fungus
The birch polypore was often called 'razor strop fungus', as its leathery flesh was once used for sharpening blades. Tiny slivers of birch polypore flesh are still used for mounting insects in museum showcases.

BIRCH POLYPORE
Piptoporus betulinus
H 2–5cm, W 8–25 × 5–20cm. Crust soft, leathery, pale, grey-brown in colour. Flesh and pores white. Very common. Fr 5–11; Wd; W.

PROJECT

Find a dead birch which has young fruitbodies of birch polypore. These are whitish, pear-shaped, and about the size of a walnut. Follow their development through a whole year, or more if possible. The brackets will grow, mature and finally decay. You may well see other fungi develop on the pore surface of the dead, rotting brackets.

MANY-ZONED POLYPORE
Trametes versicolor
H 2–6mm, W 27 × 1–5cm. Upperside velvety when young, with coloured zones of brown and grey. Pores whitish. Very common.
Fr 1–12; DWd, P, H; W.

VIOLET CONIFER BRACKET
Trichaptum abietinum
H 5mm, W 3–6 × 1–2.5cm. Grows in dense rows; upper surface hairy, with violet pores beneath. Common.
Fr 1–12; CWd; W.

BLUSHING BRACKET
Daedaleopsis confragosa
H 2–5cm, W 5–15 × 5–10cm. Upper surface yellow-brown at first, later red-brown. Pores bruise red. Common.
Fr 1–12; DWd, M; W.

BITTER BRACKET
Tyromyces stipticus
H 1–4cm, W 3–12 × 2–5cm. Almost pure white in colour, with soft, watery flesh. Common. Fr 6–12; Wd; W.

BRACKET FUNGI 3

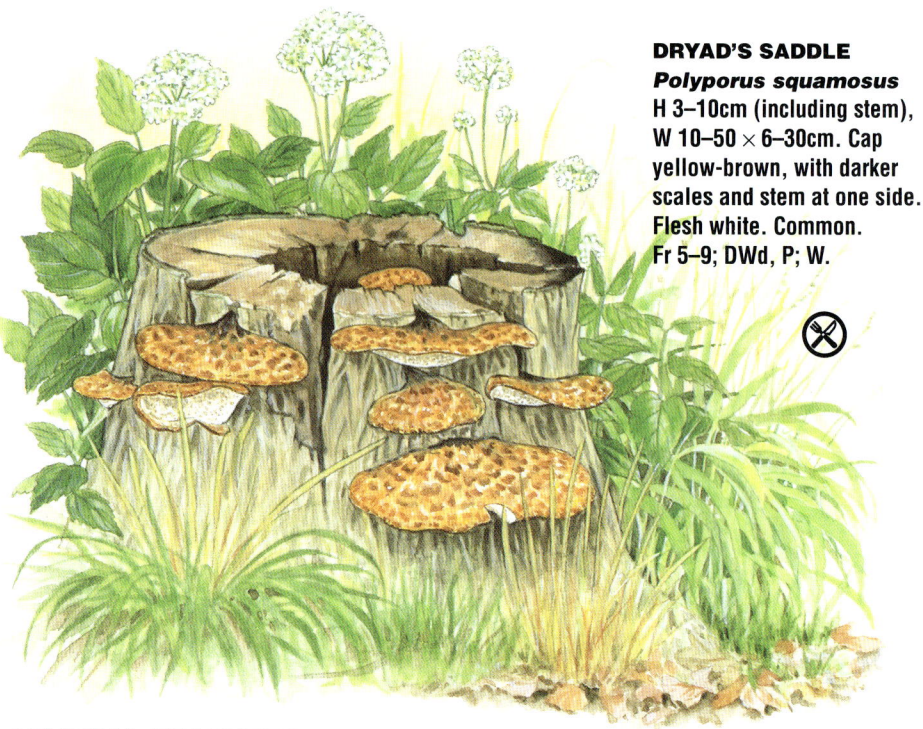

DRYAD'S SADDLE
Polyporus squamosus
H 3–10cm (including stem),
W 10–50 × 6–30cm. Cap
yellow-brown, with darker
scales and stem at one side.
Flesh white. Common.
Fr 5–9; DWd, P; W.

GENERAL FEATURES

All species shown here, except for grey fire-bracket, are annual – they complete their life cycle in one year. Species of *Polyporus* (two are shown here) are unusual amongst bracket fungi in having a stem, while Dryad's saddle and giant polypore are soft-fleshed, unlike the very tough grey fire-bracket.

HABITATS

Alder bracket, a parasite (see pp.8–9) that eventually kills its host, grows commonly on alder and more rarely on birch and hazel. Grey fire-bracket, also a parasite, is less specialised, although it is found most often on willow. It also kills its host, but more slowly than alder bracket. The rest of these fungi occur on the dead wood of deciduous trees.

The tuberous polypore (*Polyporus tuberaster*) is similar to Dryad's saddle but smaller. It grows from a large, hard, blackish tuber buried in the soil. It used to be known as the 'mushroom stone' in Italy, where it was cultivated.

GIANT POLYPORE ▼
Meripilus giganteus
H 5–20cm, W 20–80cm.
Made up of many, fused,
yellow-brown brackets at
base of trees and stumps.
Bruises black. Frequent.
Fr 7–11; DWd, P; W.

GREY FIRE-BRACKET ▲
Phellinus igniarius
H 4–15cm, W 5–15 ×
3–10cm. Cap grey, smooth,
with concentric ridges; edge
pale brown. Occasional.
Fr 1–12; DWd, H; W.

VARIED POLYPORE ▼
Polyporus varius
H 1–3cm (including stem),
W 2–8cm. Stem blackish
near base; cap smooth,
yellow-brown. Frequent.
Fr 5–10; DWd, P; W.

ALDER BRACKET ▲
Inonotus radiatus
H 1–2cm, W 2–9 × 1–5cm.
Found in tiers on trunks. Cap
with yellow edge; pores
yellow-brown. Common.
Fr 1–12; DWd, M; W.

HOW TO FIND

Alders grow on wet, rich soil,
either in large areas called carrs, or
along river banks. Find a local site
with plenty of alders and look for
alder brackets on dead or dying,
standing trunks. This fungus has a
felty surface when young and
yellow-brown pores which
characteristically reflect light when
the bracket is turned over.

BRACKET FUNGI 4

GENERAL FEATURES
The brackets shown here include two soft-fleshed, bright-coloured polypores, and some tough brackets that do not have pores. Many kinds of bracket fungi lack pores – often, they have a skin-like part as well as the bracket, and sometimes the bracket is not developed at all. Some species of *Stereum* are remarkable in 'bleeding' or turning red when scratched.

HABITATS
Most species of *Stereum* and *Hymenochaete* grow on only one or a few host trees. Some are weak parasites and others can cause damage to stored timber by rotting and staining the wood. Chicken-of-the-woods and beefsteak fungus often grow on living trees, but can also be found on dead stumps.

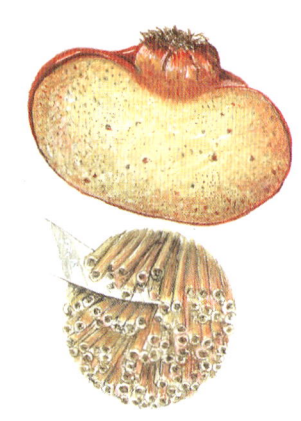

The spore-producing tubes of the beefsteak fungus are not fused together – with care, they can actually be separated from each other. This unusual characteristic is not found in any other bracket fungus.

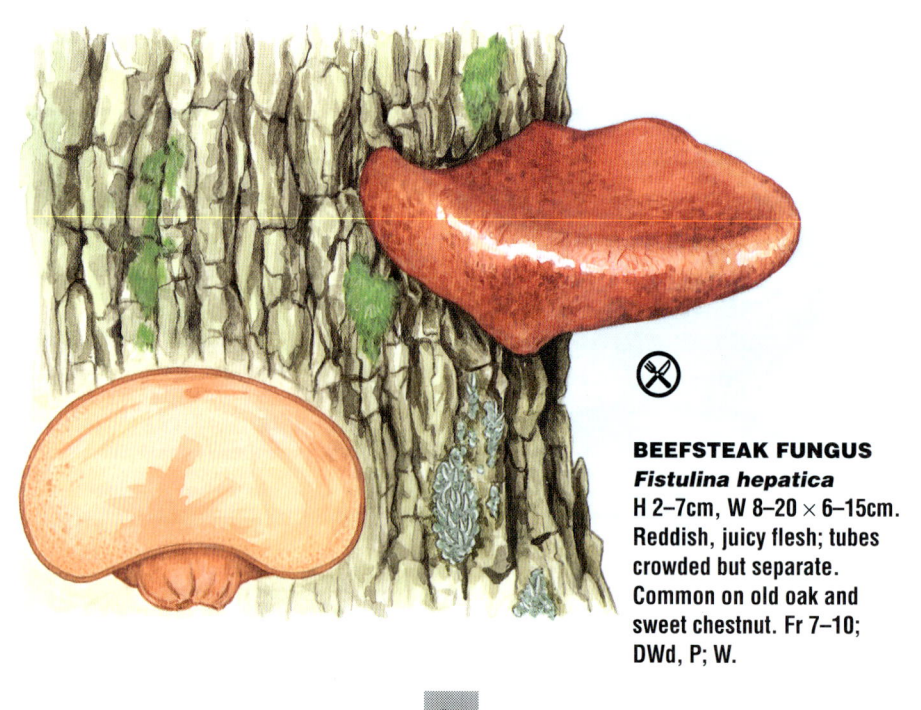

BEEFSTEAK FUNGUS
Fistulina hepatica
H 2–7cm, W 8–20 × 6–15cm.
Reddish, juicy flesh; tubes crowded but separate. Common on old oak and sweet chestnut. Fr 7–10; DWd, P; W.

CONIFER LEATHER-BRACKET ▶
Stereum sanguinolentum
H 1–2mm, W 1–4 × 0.5–1cm. Mostly skin-like, with small, hairy caps. Edge white, underside yellow-brown, 'bleeding' when scratched. Common. Fr 1–12; CWd; W.

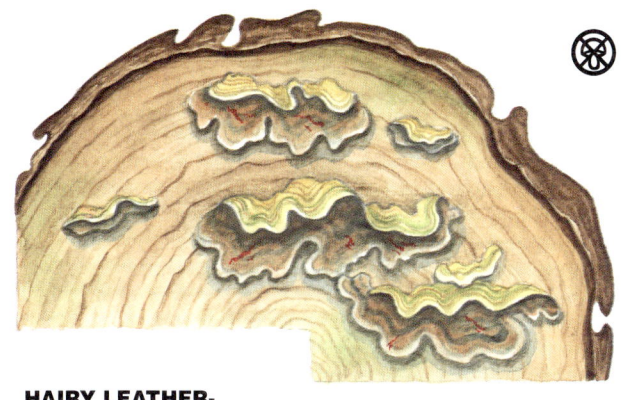

HAIRY LEATHER-BRACKET ▶
Stereum hirsutum
H 2–3mm, W 2–8 × 0.5–4cm. Cap hairy, yellow-orange, zoned. Underneath yellow at first, later orange-brown. Very common. Fr 1–12; DWd, P, H; W.

CHICKEN-OF-THE-WOODS ◀
Laetiporus sulphureus
H 5–20cm, W 10–40 × 5–25cm. Tiers of uneven, bright yellow to orange brackets. Whitish and crumbly when old. Common, on deciduous trees and yew. Fr 5–9; DWd, P, H; W.

RIGID LEATHER-BRACKET ▶
Hymenochaete rubiginosa
H 2–3mm, W 2–8 × 1–3cm. Rigid, reddish-brown brackets with skin-like part. Underside with tiny bristles; upper surface zoned. Frequent on old oak stumps. Fr 1–12; DWd, P; W.

FAIRY-CLUBS & EARTH-FANS 1

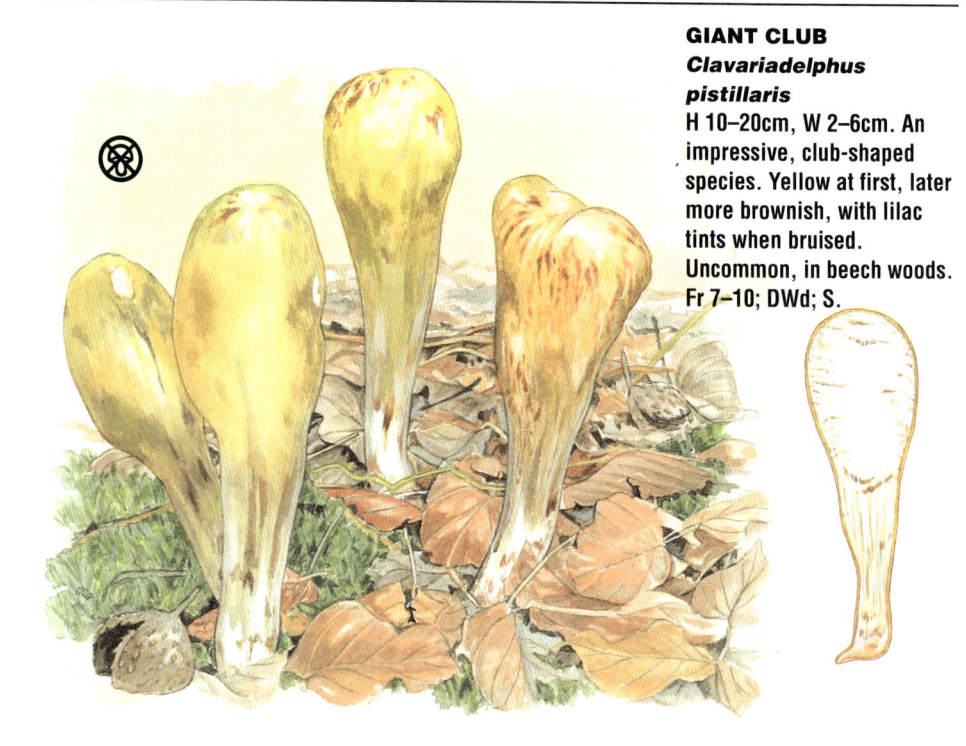

GIANT CLUB
Clavariadelphus pistillaris
H 10–20cm, W 2–6cm. An impressive, club-shaped species. Yellow at first, later more brownish, with lilac tints when bruised. Uncommon, in beech woods.
Fr 7–10; DWd; S.

GENERAL FEATURES

There are many kinds of fairy-club fungi. Some are simple, while others are tufted or branched into complex shapes. They vary in size from a few millimetres to many centimetres, and their flesh may be brittle or tough but never jelly-like. Fairy-clubs are often brightly coloured. A stem is usually present and spores are produced over the rest of the surface. The species shown here have a white spore deposit.

HABITATS

Several of these fungi are characteristic of open habitats such as grassland and dunes, while others grow amongst leaf litter in damp woods. Some smaller species grow on dead stems and leaves, but many are found on soil.

Many coral-fungi grow only in ancient woodland, often on alkaline soil. Others occur in unimproved meadows. Such habitats are increasingly under threat and some species, like this purple coral (*Clavaria zollingeri*), are now becoming scarce or are endangered.

CRESTED CORAL-FUNGUS
Clavulina cristata
H 2–6cm, W 5–10mm at base
White or cream, much branched and finely fringed at the tips. Common.
Fr 8–11; DWd; S.

HEATH FAIRY-CLUB
Clavaria argillacea
H 2–5cm, W 2–6mm. Pale yellowish or clay-brown club with brighter yellow base. Found singly or in groups, amongst moss on sandy soil. Frequent.
Fr 8–12; D, Hl; S.

WHITE SPINDLES
Clavaria vermicularis
H 4–12cm, W 3–6cm. White, pointed clubs; very fragile. Grows in tufts in grassy places. Uncommon. Fr 8–11; Md, DWd; S.

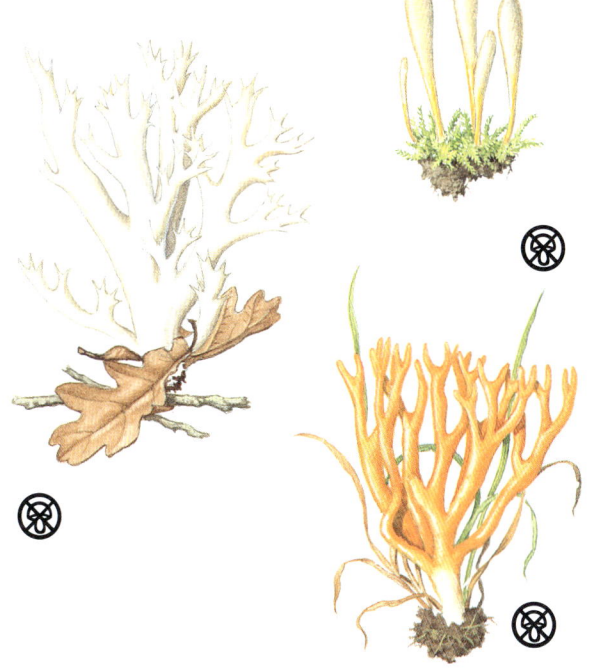

MEADOW CORAL-FUNGUS
Clavulinopsis corniculata
H 2–7cm, W 2–8mm at base. Egg-yellow, branched, with forking tips; often fused at base. Occasional to frequent.
Fr 8–11; Md, DWd; S.

HOW TO FIND

Moist ditch banks are often good places to look for many species of fairy-club fungi. Look closely and move away the overhanging vegetation to find crested coral-fungus (shown here) and various other small species that are all-too-often overlooked.

FAIRY-CLUBS & EARTH-FANS 2

GENERAL FEATURES
Some fairy-clubs have a yellowish spore deposit. These belong in the large *Ramaria* genus and are usually much branched and fleshy – two *Ramaria* species are shown here. Cauliflower fungus is not closely related, but could be seen as a specialised fairy-club with branches flattened into lobes. Earth-fans vary in shape; some are coral-like but others are fan-shaped or skin-like. They have purple-brown, warted spores and are related to some kinds of tooth fungi.

HABITATS
The fungi shown here are woodland species, occurring in litter or on wood. Cauliflower fungus is a parasite, mainly on pine, and common earth-fan can damage conifer seedlings.

Fairy-clubs belonging to the genus *Ramaria* are usually much-branched and commonly known as coral-fungi. There are about 40 species known in northern Europe. Many of these – including this one, *Ramaria decurrens* – are now rare.

STRAIGHT CORAL-FUNGUS
Ramaria stricta
H 4–10cm, W 3–7cm (whole fungus). Much-branched; branches straight, with yellow tips. Grows on sticks and stumps. Occasional to frequent. Fr 8–11; DWd; W.

▲ **COMMON EARTH-FAN**
Thelephora terrestris
H 1–2cm, W 2–6cm. Grows in fan-like clusters. Cap fibrous with fringed edge. Underside clay-brown with paler edge. Common, especially with conifers on sandy soil. Fr 7–11; CWd, Hl, DWd; L, W.

PROJECT

Various groups of fungi include species with club-shaped fruitbodies, although they may not necessarily be related to the fairy-clubs. A common example is jelly antler fungus. Find examples of this and a fairy-club such as meadow coral-fungus and compare their texture and structure. One obvious difference you will notice is that the jelly antler fungus is far more flexible than the fairy-club species.

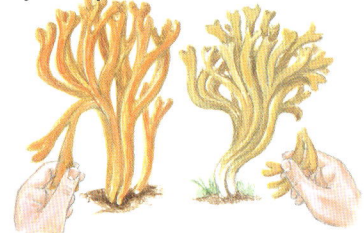

Calocera viscosa

Clavulinopsis corniculata

OCHRE-GREEN ▷
CORAL-FUNGUS
Ramaria abietina
H 3–6cm, W 3–4cm (whole fungus). Much-branched; branches olive-brown, more greenish when dry. Felty white base. Occasional. Fr 7–10; CWd; L.

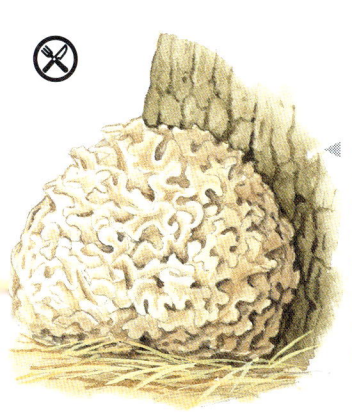

◀ **CAULIFLOWER FUNGUS**
Sparassis crispa
H 10–20cm, W 20–50cm. Like a sponge or cauliflower in appearance. Root parasite, found at base of conifer trunks. Occasional to frequent. Fr 8–10; CWd; W.

▲ **CABBAGE EARTH-FAN**
Thelephora palmata
H 3–8cm, W 2–4cm (whole fungus). Upright, flattened branches; grey-brown. Smells strongly of rotten cabbage. Uncommon. Fr 8–11; CWd; L.

CHANTERELLES & TOOTH FUNGI

HEDGEHOG FUNGUS
Hydnum repandum
H 3–8cm, CW 3–15cm, SW 1–4cm. Cap cream to pale yellowish, smooth; underside with spines. Stem paler. Common. Fr 7–11; DWd, CWd; S.

GENERAL FEATURES

These fungi are characterised by the form of their spore-producing surface. In chanterelles, this is smooth or veined, whereas in tooth fungi it is covered with spines. Tooth fungi are actually a mixture of species from several families, not necessarily closely related. Two of these families are represented here. Chanterelles, in contrast, are all members of a single family.

HABITATS

These are woodland fungi, growing on soil or litter. Many, including the true chanterelles and some tooth fungi, are mycorrhizal (see pp.8–9), growing in association with various trees; others live on dead or decaying matter. Soil type is important for many species; some, such as horn-of-plenty, require a nutrient-rich soil but others prefer sandy, acid conditions. Ear pick-fungus is unique in this group in growing on fallen, often buried, cones of conifers.

The term tooth-fungi covers a range of unrelated species which have in common spines or teeth on which spores are produced. Some, such as species of *Hydnum*, are fleshy and edible. Others, such as *Hydnellum* (shown here) and *Phellodon*, are tough and fibrous. Because of pollution, many of these are becoming rare.

TRUMPET CHANTERELLE
Cantharellus tubaeformis
H 3–8cm, CW 2–5cm, SW 4–10mm. Brownish cap; underside with thick, forking, greyish veins. Stem yellow. Frequent. Fr 8–10; CWd, DWd; S.

HORN-OF-PLENTY
Craterellus cornucopioides
H 6–12cm, W 2–8cm. Trumpet-like, hollow to the base. Outer surface grey; inner surface blackish-brown, slightly scaly. In clumps in leaf litter. Occasional. Fr 8–11; DWd; S.

CHANTERELLE
Cantharellus cibarius
H 5–10cm, CW 2–10cm, SW 0.5–2cm. Entirely egg yellow; underside of cap with thick, forking veins. A much sought-after edible fungus. Frequent. Fr 6–10; CWd, DWd; S.

EAR PICK-FUNGUS
Auriscalpium vulgare
H 3–7cm, CW 1–2cm, SW 2–4mm. Cap brown, felty, with spines underneath. Stem brown, hairy. Grows on fallen pine cones. Frequent, easily overlooked. Fr 1–12; CWd; L.

ODDS AND ENDS

SHOOTING DUNG-FUNGUS
Pilobolus sp.
H 2–10mm, W 0.1–0.9mm.
Glassy, upright structure with black spore mass at the top. This is shot away onto vegetation which is then eaten by grazing animals. Very common. Fr 1–12; Dg.

GENERAL FEATURES

A variety of common or characteristic, but often neglected, fungi are shown here. One of the larger slime moulds, flowers of tan, is also included. Slime moulds are not true fungi, although most are fungus-like when mature.

HABITATS

The species shown illustrate some of the wide range of habitats that are colonised by fungi. Brush moulds grow where they can easily get the sugars they need; bread and fruit are ideal. Species of *Pilobolus* thrive only on dung. The powdery pupa fungus is an example of the many fungi which kill and grow on insects. Horny substances such as hair and nails are difficult to break down, but specialised fungi such as hoof fungus can even live on these.

There are many interesting associations between fungi and other organisms. One example involves an eelworm and *Pilobolus*. The eelworm causes a lung disease of cows and uses *Pilobolus* as part of its life cycle. The eelworm larva crawls up onto the spore ball and is shot off with it onto the grass. It is eaten by cattle and eventually develops in their lungs.

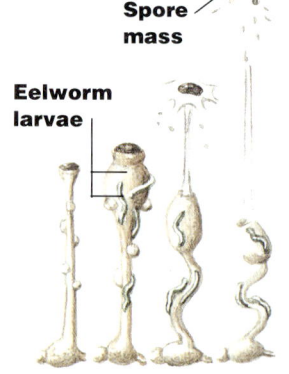

Spore mass

Eelworm larvae

HOOF FUNGUS
Onygena equina
H 2–10mm, CW 2–4mm.
Slender stalk, roundish head.
In clusters on rotting horns
and hooves. Occasional.
Fr 1–12.

BRUSH FUNGI
Penicillium sp.
Blue or green moulds, very
common in various habitats,
including on food. Also used
for cheese flavouring and in
medicine.

FLOWERS OF TAN
Fuligo septica
H 4–10mm, W 3–15cm. At
first yellow, slimy; dark,
powdery spore mass later.
Common. Fr 6–11; Wd, Hl, P,
W, H; W, L.

PROJECT
Investigate how far the spore balls of shooting dung-fungi are shot. Find some fresh dung of horse or deer. Wearing rubber gloves, place some on moist tissue in closed containers of different heights. Only the container lids should be see-through, so that light enters from above. Leave for a day or so until the fungi appear. The spore balls will be shot upwards. Do they reach the lids of all the containers or just some of them?

POWDERY PUPA FUNGUS
Paecilomyces farinosus
H 5–30mm, W 2–5mm.
White, powdery upper part,
yellowish stem. Common on
dead insects such as moth
caterpillars. Fr 6–11.

BOLETES 1

DOTTED-STEM BOLETE
Boletus erythropus
H 8–18cm, CW 6–20cm, SW 3–6cm. Dark brown cap and red pores; stem with red dots. Flesh quickly turns blue when cut. Common. Fr 6–10; Wd; S.

GENERAL FEATURES

Boletes as a group are very distinctive. Like agarics, they have short-lived, fleshy fruitbodies, but their spores develop in tubes rather than gills. The flesh of many species changes colour when bruised or cut. The stem may be smooth but is more often covered with net-like veins, dots or scales.

HABITATS

Most boletes are woodland fungi and grow in mycorrhizal association (see pp.8–9) with trees. Many bolete species can grow with a variety of trees, although some are more specific, living only with one particular species. A few boletes grow on wood, and one (*Boletus parasiticus*) grows only as a parasite on the common earthball.

Boletes suffer from many parasites. They are often infested with maggots or midge larvae, but perhaps the worst parasite is a fungus called *Sepedonium chrysospermum*, seen here. This rots the fungus and, when mature, develops a yellow, powdery mass of spores.

RED-CRACKED BOLETE
Boletus chrysenteron
H 4–8cm CW 3–10cm, SW 1–2cm. Cap velvety at first, cracking to show red underneath. Stem red; pores yellow, slowly blueing when bruised. Common.
Fr 7–11; DWd; S.

PENNY BUN
Boletus edulis
H 10–20cm, CW 8–25cm, SW 3–8cm. Also called cep. Stem with pale network at top; flesh white. Excellent edible fungus. Common.
Fr 7–11; Wd; S.

PARASITIC BOLETE
Boletus parasiticus
H 2–7cm, CW 2–5cm, SW 5–15mm. Yellow-brown cap, pores yellowish, stem yellow or red. Parasite on common earthball. Occasional.
Fr 7–10; Wd.

BITTER BOLETE
Tylopilus felleus
H 8–15cm, CW 5–15cm, SW 2–5cm. Tubes pinkish; stem with coarse, dark network. Flesh white, very bitter. Frequent. Fr 6–10; Wd; S.

BOLETES 2

GENERAL FEATURES
The boletes shown here have some special and distinctive features. Species of *Leccinum* have tall stems which are covered with small scales, whilst *Suillus* species have characteristically slimy caps. The old man of the woods is unique amongst European boletes in having a cap covered with coarse scales.

HABITATS
Leccinum species are mycorrhizal (see pp.8–9); they usually grow with deciduous trees, and each species usually occurs with only one kind of tree. *Suillus* species are also often restricted to a single partner but, in contrast, occur only with coniferous trees.

One distinctive characteristic of boletes is that, unlike bracket fungi, the spore-producing tube layer can easily be peeled away from the cap flesh.

ORANGE BIRCH BOLETE
Leccinum versipelle
H 10–20cm, CW 6–20cm, SW 1–4cm. Large, with orange cap and dark, scaly stem. Common, with birch.
Fr 7–10; Wd; S.

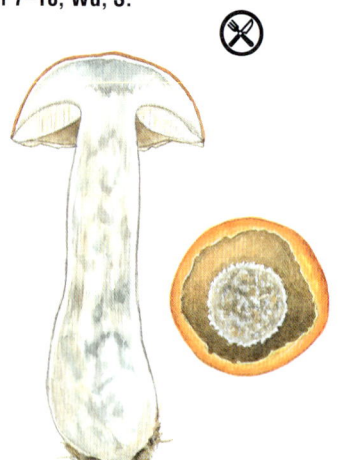

BROWN BIRCH BOLETE
Leccinum scabrum
H 8–15cm, CW 5–15cm, SW 1–3cm. Brown cap; stem with brown scales; flesh soft, white. Common. Fr 6–10; Wd; S.

SLIPPERY JACK
Suillus luteus
H 5–10cm, CW 4–10cm, SW 1–3cm. Dark, slimy, purple-brown cap; top of stem yellow with darker dots; well-developed ring present. Common, with pine. Fr 8–11; CWd; S.

LARCH BOLETE
Suillus grevillei
H 6–10cm, CW 3–10cm, SW 1–2cm. Cap yellow or orange-brown; stem with ring. Common, under larch. Fr 7–10; Wd; S.

OLD MAN OF THE WOODS
Strobilomyces strobilaceus
H 7–15cm, CW 5–12cm, SW 1–3cm. Unique and easily recognised. Flesh reddens when cut. Infrequent. Fr 7–10; Wd; S, W.

PROJECT

Scaly-stemmed boletes are good subjects for painting. They are often brightly coloured, and the flesh of many species also develops a range of colours when cut. These colours are important when identifying species. Find some specimens and make water-colour paintings of them.

ROLL-RIMS AND SPIKE-CAPS

GENERAL FEATURES

Roll-rims and spike-caps are considered to be relatives of the boletes, although their spores are produced in gills rather than tubes. Spike-caps have black spores and a slimy cap, unlike roll-rims which are brown-spored and usually dry. False chanterelle is not strictly a member of this group. Although it shares some characteristics with roll-rims, its spore deposit is white.

HABITATS

These fungi grow mostly in woods. Some grow in mycorrhizal association (see pp.8–9) with trees, whilst others occur on rotten wood and litter. Rosy spike-cap is a parasite which grows on the mycorrhizal roots developed by pine and the bolete *Suillus bovinus*. The fruitbodies of these two fungi are often found together.

Brown roll-rim was once considered to be edible, but is now known to cause severe and even fatal kidney failure in some people.

BROWN ROLL-RIM
Paxillus involutus
H 4–7cm, CW 4–12cm, SW 5–15mm. Cap has woolly edge, characteristically rolled inwards. Gills bruise rapidly dark brown. Very common. Fr 7–11; Wd, P; S, W.

FALSE CHANTERELLE
Hygrophoropsis aurantiacus
H 3–6cm, CW 2–7cm, SW 5–8mm. Cap yellow-orange with inrolled edge. Gills orange, forked, arching down the stem. Very common. Fr 8–11; Wd; S.

ROSY SPIKE-CAP
Gomphidius roseus
H 3–5cm, CW 3–5cm, SW 4–10mm. A beautiful fungus, with a red, slimy cap and gills which arch down the stem. Uncommon. Fr 8–10; CWd; S.

VELVET ROLL-RIM
Paxillus atrotomentosus
H 3–8cm, CW 10–30cm, SW 2–5cm. Cap dark brown, domed; flesh cream; stem dark brown and velvety. Frequent. Fr 7–11; CWd; W.

VISCID SPIKE-CAP
Gomphidius glutinosus
H 4–10cm, CW 4–10cm, SW 1–2cm. Stem looks thickened below the gills due to remains of the veil. Stem yellowish at base. Occasional, on sandy soil. Fr 7–10; CWd; S.

OYSTER FUNGI AND ALLIES

OYSTER MUSHROOM
Pleurotus ostreatus
CW 5–15cm, SL 0–4cm. Cap blue-grey; gills white. In tiers on trunks or logs. Common. Fr 9–4; DWd, P; W.

GENERAL FEATURES

Toadstools that have bracket-like fruitbodies, with short stems usually attached at the side of the cap, are commonly called oyster fungi. They do not form a natural group, but include a variety of unrelated species. Those shown here have white spores and belong to two families. Bonfire chanterelle, although not a typical oyster fungus, is regarded as a relative of *Pleurotus* and is therefore also included.

HABITATS

Most oyster fungi grow on rotten wood, with a few occurring as weak parasites on unhealthy trees. Some of the smaller species grow on herbs and mosses. Bonfire chanterelle is an exception – it can only be found on old fire sites. Most species appear during the autumn, sometimes late in the season, although a few can be found in the summer. Oyster mushroom is able to survive the frost, and can often be found throughout the winter.

Oyster mushrooms belonging to the genus *Pleurotus* are often good to eat. Several species are now specially grown on compressed straw or sterilised logs, then sold in shops and supermarkets.

BONFIRE CHANTERELLE
Faerberia carbonaria
H 3–6cm, CW 1–5cm, SW 5–10mm. Greyish, funnel-shaped cap. Grows in clusters on burnt ground. Scarce. Fr 8–11; Wd, P; B.

VEILED OYSTER
Pleurotus dryinus
CW 5–15cm, SW 1–3cm, SL 2–6cm. Cap pale grey, felty, often with remains of veil at the edge; gills whitish. Stem with ring which soon disappears. Occasional. Fr 8–12; Wd, P; W.

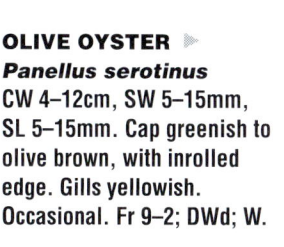

OLIVE OYSTER
Panellus serotinus
CW 4–12cm, SW 5–15mm, SL 5–15mm. Cap greenish to olive brown, with inrolled edge. Gills yellowish. Occasional. Fr 9–2; DWd; W.

HOW TO FIND

Go out into a beech wood in late November or early December and examine any old, damaged trees or fallen, rotting trunks that you come across. If you are lucky, you will discover the beautiful, grey-blue tiers of oyster mushroom (*Pleurotus ostreatus*). Look for other species of oyster fungi on the same trunks, or on wood of other trees.

WAX-CAPS

GENERAL FEATURES
Many of the wax-caps are brightly coloured and attractive. Some are slimy on the surface, and several species have a distinctive smell. Others are dry or fragile fungi and they are classified into several different groups. All species have white spores and thick gills. A veil is present in one group, but this is slimy and does not leave a ring on the stem.

HABITATS
Many of the brightly coloured wax-caps are found in untreated, natural meadows, others occur in boggy places or in dunes. Sometimes they grow mixed with earth-tongues, pink-gills and fairy-clubs. Related fungi occur in woods and are mycorrhizal (see pp.8–9). These are mostly white or dull-coloured species.

Wax-cap odours
Some wax-caps have a strong, distinctive smell. *Hygrocybe russocoriaceus* is a white, grassland species with a strong, fragrant smell often described as 'Russian leather'. Goat-moth wax-cap (*Hygrophorus cossus*) grows in beech woods and has a strong, unpleasant smell like goat moth caterpillars. Almond wax-cap (*H. agathosmus*) has a striking, pleasant smell of bitter almond.

BLACKENING WAX-CAP
Hygrocybe conica
H 3–8cm, CW 1–5cm, SW 3–10mm. Reddish-orange, cone-shaped cap, and yellowish or orange stem. Flesh blackens when bruised and with age. Common.
Fr 7–11; M, D, P; S.

PARROT WAX-CAP
Hygrocybe psittacina
H 2–6cm, CW 1–3cm, SW 2–5mm. Green colours are characteristic, mixed with yellow. Slimy cap and stem. Common. Fr 8–11; Md, P, DWd; S.

DUNE WAX-CAP
Hygrocybe conica var. *conicoides*
H 3–8cm, CW 1–4cm, SW 3–7mm. Similar to blackening wax-cap, but darker red and with reddish gills. Flesh blackens less when bruised. Occasional. Fr 9–12; D; S.

HERALD OF THE WINTER
Hygrophorus hypothejus
H 4–7cm, CW 2–5cm, SW 5–10mm. Olive-brown, slimy cap and yellowish colours in gills and stem. Common, with pine. Fr 10–1; CWd; S.

MEADOW WAX-CAP
Hygrocybe pratensis
H 4–9cm, CW 3–8cm, SW 5–15mm. Cap dry, pale orange-brown with raised centre; stem whitish, tapered. Frequent. Fr 9–11; Md; S.

SATIN-WHITE WAX-CAP
Hygrocybe virginea
H 3–7cm, CW 1–4cm, SW 2–6mm. White or pale cream throughout; gills arching down stem. Greasy to touch. Common. Fr 9–11; Md, P; S.

FUNNEL-CAPS AND OTHERS

GENERAL FEATURES
The fungi shown here all have white spores. Funnel-caps have gills that arch down the stem, and do not have veils. Most have no scales on the cap. Honey fungus has slightly arching gills, but it has a ring on its stem and a scaly cap. Porcelain fungus is very slimy, and broad-gilled agaric has white cords at its stem base.

HABITATS
Honey fungus is a serious parasite (see pp.8–9), often causing damage to trees in gardens and parks. The other species shown here are saprobes (see pp.8–9), although porcelain fungus, which grows on dead branches of beech, can be a weak parasite. Funnel-caps are woodland or grassland fungi, growing in troops or fairy rings.

Honey fungus spreads by characteristic, flattened, bootlace-like structures called rhizomorphs. These have a black rind and a white flesh and are easy to recognise. They can grow under bark or in soil.

HONEY FUNGUS
Armillaria mellea
H 6–15cm, CW 3–12cm, SW 5–15mm. Yellowish brown cap with small scales; stem pale yellowish or brown, with woolly ring. Very common, growing in large tufts. Fr 7–12; Wd, P, H; W.

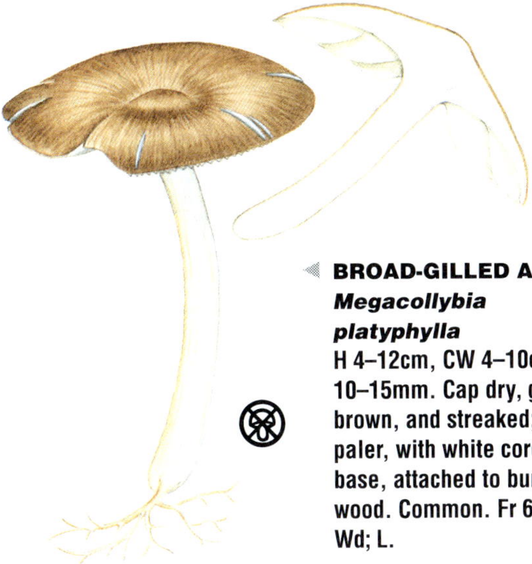

CLUB-FOOTED FUNNEL-CAP
Clitocybe clavipes
H 4–8cm, CW 4–7cm, SW 10–15mm. Cap grey-brown; gills creamy white, arching down stem; stem thicker at base. Frequent. Fr 8–11; Wd; S, L.

BROAD-GILLED AGARIC
Megacollybia platyphylla
H 4–12cm, CW 4–10cm, SW 10–15mm. Cap dry, grey-brown, and streaked; stem paler, with white cords at base, attached to buried wood. Common. Fr 6–10; Wd; L.

PORCELAIN FUNGUS
Oudemansiella mucida
H 3–10cm, CW 2–8cm, SW 3–7mm. An unmistakeable fungus, with partly see-through, slimy cap and ring on stem. In tufts on beech. Frequent. Fr 7–10; DWd; W.

BLUE-GREEN FUNNEL-CAP
Clitocybe odora
H 4–7cm, CW 3–7cm, SW 4–8mm. Attractive grey-blue colours in cap and stem, fading with age; gills paler. Smells strongly of aniseed. Frequent. Fr 8–11; Wd; S.

NAVEL-CAPS

ORANGE NAVEL-CAP
Rickenella fibula
H 2–5cm, CW 4–10mm, SW 1–2mm. Orange cap with white gills; stem orange, covered with tiny hairs. Common. Fr 6–11; M.

GENERAL FEATURES
These are mostly small and delicate fungi with gills that arch down the stem and white spores. They have no ring or volva. Often the caps are depressed at the centre, giving the group its common name. Navel-caps belong to several different groups, and they vary considerably in colour and in microscopic characteristics.

HABITATS
Several of these fungi grow with mosses and liverworts – *Sphagnum* bogs are a good place to look for them. Some are parasitic on mosses, although apparently cause them little harm. Other species occur on heathlands or in dunes, and one is found commonly on burnt ground.

Some navel-caps grow in special association with algae, forming green, scale-like or granular structures on wet turf. These are only easy to find when the navel-cap produces its fruitbodies.

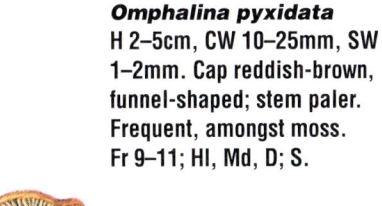

HEATH NAVEL-CAP
Omphalina pyxidata
H 2–5cm, CW 10–25mm, SW 1–2mm. Cap reddish-brown, funnel-shaped; stem paler. Frequent, amongst moss.
Fr 9–11; Hl, Md, D; S.

BONFIRE NAVEL-CAP
Myxomphalia maura
H 3–5cm, CW 1–4cm, SW 2–3mm. Cap with deep 'navel', grey-brown, striate. Occasional. Fr 8–11; Wd, Hl, P; B.

EYE-SPOT NAVEL-CAP
Rickenella swartzii
H 2–5cm, CW 4–10mm, SW 1–2mm. Cap with dark violet centre; stem dark at top, covered with tiny hairs. Frequent. Fr 6–11; M.

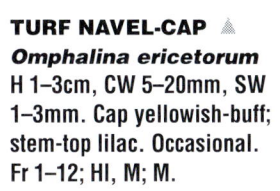

TURF NAVEL-CAP
Omphalina ericetorum
H 1–3cm, CW 5–20mm, SW 1–3mm. Cap yellowish-buff; stem-top lilac. Occasional.
Fr 1–12; Hl, M; M.

HOW TO FIND

The eye-spot navel-cap and orange navel-cap (shown here) are probably the easiest of these species to find. They are small but distinctive and easy to see on the green background provided by the moss on which they grow. They can be found on most mossy lawns and often occur in groups. Various kinds of pixy-caps and bonnet-caps may grow with them.

BONNET-CAPS

OAK BONNET-CAP
Mycena inclinata
H 5–12cm, CW 1–4cm, SW 2–4cm. Stem reddish-yellow in lower part, with felty, whitish base. Cap with finely grooved edge; gills white. Smell rancid or oily. Frequent; in tufts, especially on oak. Fr 9–12; DWd, P; W.

GENERAL FEATURES

These are mostly small and delicate toadstools which lack veils, have white spores and a bell- or bonnet-shaped cap. They vary greatly in colour, although many are greyish. Some are slimy, and a few have a white or coloured juice. Many have a characteristic smell, providing an important clue for identification. They may be solitary, sometimes in troops, or grow in large clumps or tufts.

HABITATS

Bonnet-caps mainly occur amongst leaf litter or in grass or moss, although some grow on dead stumps or trunks. Most species are very specific in their requirements, growing only in a particular habitat.

Some bonnet-caps have a white or red to carrot-coloured juice. Orange-staining bonnet-cap (*Mycena crocata*), shown here, occurs in beech woods. Large bleeding bonnet-cap (*Mycena haematopus*) has red juice and grows in various habitats.

PROJECT

Many common bonnet-caps have a distinctive smell. Some species smell of radishes, others smell of chlorine or meal. Some smells can be detected in the field, but it is better to place the fungus in a small, closed container for a while so that the odour is more concentrated. In some species, the smell becomes stronger as the fruitbody dries.

MARRAM BONNET-CAP
Mycena chlorantha
H 3–6cm, CW 8–15mm, SW 1–2mm. Cap greenish; stem greyish. Smell chemical. Frequent, on marram grass.
Fr 9–12; D; L.

BLACK BONNET-CAP
Mycena leucogala
H 4–10cm, CW 8–20mm, SW 2–3mm. Blackish-brown with pale grey gills; stem with milky fluid. Common.
Fr 8–11; DWd, P, Hl, D; S, B.

COMMON DISC-FOOT
Mycena stylobates
H 2–5cm, CW 3–8mm, SW 0.5–1mm. Pale grey to whitish; stem with disc-like base up to 4mm across. Frequent. Fr 7–11; Wd, P; L.

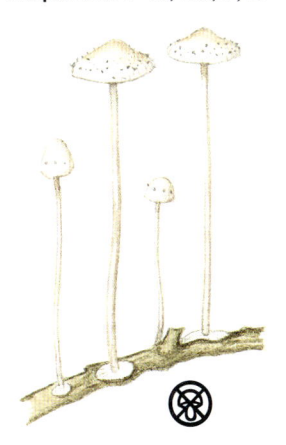

LILAC BONNET-CAP
Mycena pura
H 5–12cm, CW 1–4cm, SW 3–6mm. Usually pink or lilac throughout. Smells strongly of radishes. Common.
Fr 8–11; Wd, Hl, P; S, L.

DECEIVERS AND OTHERS

GENERAL FEATURES
These are mostly tough and fibrous fungi that have white spores and lack veils. Species of *Laccaria* are popularly known as 'deceivers' because they vary so much in appearance. Most are violet- or lilac-coloured. Species of *Marasmius* can be quite fleshy, as in fairy ring champignon, or very thin-fleshed and slender, as in the horse-hair fungus. Most can revive after drying out.

Threads for jewellery
Some species of *Marasmius* form wiry, black strands by which the fungus spreads. These strands are often referred to as 'horse hairs'. In South America, birds are known to use these strands for nest building. The strands are also used by some people to tie jewellery.

HABITATS
Deceivers, among the most common woodland fungi, usually form mycorrhizal associations with trees (see pp.8–9). *Marasmius* species are mostly saprobes (see pp.8–9), although some parasitic species are known. Many are found on decaying leaves and stems.

FAIRY RING CHAMPIGNON
Marasmius oreades
H 3–7cm, CW 2–5cm, SW 3–6mm. Cap yellowish brown; gills paler than cap; stem tough, downy. Very common, in fairy rings.
Fr 6–10; Md, G, P; S.

PROJECT

Fairy rings, mostly formed by *Marasmius oreades*, are a common sight on lawns and in fields. Examine one carefully in autumn, when the toadstools are growing, and note the difference in vegetation growth inside the ring, around the ring's edge, and outside the ring.

LITTLE WHEEL TOADSTOOL
Marasmius rotula
H 2–6cm, CW 5–15mm, SW 0.5–1mm. Cap like tiny, whitish parachute; gills attached to collar around stem, like spokes of wheel; stem blackish below. Common. Fr 6–10; Wd, P; L.

THE DECEIVER
Laccaria laccata
H 4–10cm, CW 1–4cm, SW 0.3–0.7mm. Variable, although always pinkish with thick gills. Very common. Fr 7–11; Wd, P, M; S.

AMETHYST DECEIVER
Laccaria amethystea
H 4–8cm, CW 2–5cm, SW 4–8mm. Beautiful violet colours throughout. Very common. Fr 8–11; Wd; S.

HORSE-HAIR FUNGUS
Marasmius androsaceus
H 2–6cm, CW 4–10mm, SW 0.5–1mm. Cap pinkish brown; gills paler; stem black, hair-like. Very common, especially on heather stems and conifer needles. Fr 6–10; Wd, Hl; L.

TOUGH-SHANKS & GREYLINGS

SPINDLE SHANK
Collybia fusipes
H 5–10cm, CW 3–7cm, SW 1–2cm. Reddish-brown; spindle-shaped, fibrous stem. Frequent, in large tufts on roots of deciduous trees. Fr 6–11; DWd; W.

GENERAL FEATURES

The main characters of these fungi are the lack of a veil and gills that are narrowly attached to the stem. Most have white spores, but in some tough-shanks the spore deposit is yellowish. Tough-shanks have fibrous stems. Greylings are small toadstools with dull, often grey colours and are more fragile than tough-shanks.

HABITATS

These fungi grow in a wide range of habitats. Some are woodland saprobes (see pp.8–9) and grow in leaf litter, either in groups or in fairy rings. Others occur on bonfire sites, in *Sphagnum* bogs, or on decaying fungi. Velvet shank can grow on living trees; it appears late in the year and is able to survive freezing.

Four tiny, whitish species of *Collybia* grow on rotten toadstools and brackets. Three of these develop from a small tuber within the host fungus. One rare species, *Collybia racemos*a (shown here), has a stem with side branches.

VELVET SHANK
Flammulina velutipes
H 2–8cm, CW 2–7cm, SW 3–10mm. Stem velvety, dark brown towards base; cap sticky, orange-brown. Common, in tufts. Fr 10–3; DWd, P, H; W.

SPOTTED TOUGH-SHANK
Collybia maculata
H 6–12cm, CW 4–10cm, SW 5–20mm. Whitish, with red-brown spots. Gills closely spaced; flesh tough. Common. Fr 7–11; Wd; L.

SPHAGNUM GREYLING
Tephrocybe palustris
H 4–8cm, CW 1–3cm, SW 1–3mm. Cap striate to centre; stem fragile. Grows in *Sphagnum* moss. Frequent. Fr 6–10; M; M.

WOOD WOOLLY-FOOT
Collybia peronata
H 4–8cm, CW 3–6cm, SW 3–6mm. Stem tough, often yellowish, with woolly base which binds litter. Common. Fr 7–11; Wd; L.

HOW TO FIND

Most tough-shanks occur where there is plenty of leaf litter in deciduous woods. Some are common and easy to find. Visit woods in the autumn, after a wet period, and search amongst the litter. Butter cap (*Collybia butyracea*), wood tough-shank (*C. dryophila*), wood woolly-foot (shown here) and tufted tough-shank (*C. confluens*) are the commonest species.

KNIGHT-CAPS AND BLEWITS

GENERAL FEATURES

These are mostly sturdy fungi with white or pinkish spores. They all belong to a single family, but represent several different groups or genera. Knight-caps vary greatly in colour and smell. They belong to the genus *Tricholoma*, which includes many white-spored species with gills that appear to be notched on their lower edge where they meet the stem. Blewits belong to the genus *Lepista*, which have pinkish spores; several are violet or purple in colour and most have a pleasant smell.

Many knight-caps have a special gill attachment known as sinuate. This gives an S-shaped outline where the gill joins the stem.

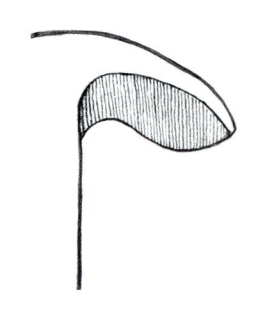

HABITATS

Knight-caps, which are mycorrhizal fungi (see pp.8–9), can be found in woods. Blewits are saprobes (see pp.8–9), growing in various habitats including woods and grassland. Plums-and-custard grows on wood.

PLUMS-AND-CUSTARD
Tricholomopsis rutilans
H 4–8cm, CW 5–12cm, SW 10–15mm. A beautiful and distinctive fungus, with purple scale on a yellow background. Gills yellow. Common. Fr 6–11; CWd; W.

SILKY-GREY KNIGHT-CAP
Tricholoma virgatum
H 5–9cm, CW 4–7cm, SW 1–2cm. Cap grey-brown, streaked with silky fibres. Stem white. Smell musty. Uncommon. Fr 8–10; CWd; S.

ST GEORGE'S MUSHROOM
Calocybe gambosa
H 4–8cm, CW 5–12cm, SW 1–2cm. Whitish throughout, sometimes with yellowish tints on cap. Frequent. Fr 4–6; P, H, G; S.

WOOD BLEWIT
Lepista nuda
H 5–10cm, CW 5–10cm, SW 1–2cm. Violet-coloured when young, later brownish. Stem swollen at base, binding leaf litter. Common. Fr 1–12; P, H, Wd; L.

SULPHUR KNIGHT-CAP
Tricholoma sulphureum
H 4–10cm, CW 3–8cm, SW 5–10mm. Yellow throughout, with a strong, unpleasant smell of coal gas. Frequent. Fr 8–10; Wd; S.

DEATH CAPS AND GRISETTES

FLY AGARIC
Amanita muscaria
H 9–20cm, CW 8–20cm, SW 10–25mm. A striking species, easily recognised by its red cap and white scales. Common. Fr 8–11; Wd; S.

GENERAL FEATURES

These are typical toadstools, with an outer veil which encloses the whole fruitbody when young. This breaks as the fruitbody grows, leaving a volva or scaly patches at the stem base, and sometimes scales on the cap. Often, there is also a ring on the stem. The caps of those species that do not have a ring are usually striped or streaked at the edge. All species have free, crowded gills and white spores.

HABITATS

Species of *Amanita* are mycorrhizal (see pp.8–9), and are mostly woodland fungi. A few occur with dwarf willow and birch in open, mountainous areas. These fungi are often quite specific, being associated with just one or a few trees. Soil conditions, whether acid or alkaline, are also important for some species.

Amanita muscaria is popularly called the fly agaric. This is because, in medieval times, it was used as a fly killer. The fungus was often ground up and added to milk or sugar, which was then set out to attract flies and other insects.

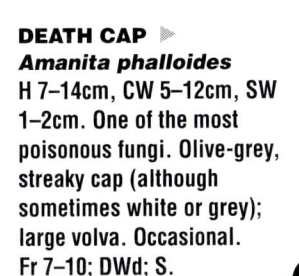

DEATH CAP
Amanita phalloides
H 7–14cm, CW 5–12cm, SW 1–2cm. One of the most poisonous fungi. Olive-grey, streaky cap (although sometimes white or grey); large volva. Occasional.
Fr 7–10; DWd; S.

TAWNY GRISETTE
Amanita fulva
H 7–12cm, CW 4–8cm, SW 8–12mm. Cap tawny brown, with striate edge; volva with tawny patches. Common.
Fr 6–10; Wd; S.

DESTROYING ANGEL
Amanita virosa
H 9–15cm, CW 5–10cm, SW 1–2cm. White throughout; stem fibrous-scaly. Related to death cap, and equally poisonous. Uncommon.
Fr 7–10; Wd; S.

THE BLUSHER
Amanita rubescens
H 6–15cm, CW 5–15cm, SW 1–3cm. Cap red-brown, with small scales; flesh white, bruising slowly reddish. Common. Fr 6–10; Wd, P; S.

PARASOLS

PARASOL MUSHROOM
Macrolepiota procera
H 15–30cm, CW 12–25cm, SW 8–15mm. Soft, scaly cap, double ring and snake-like pattern on stem. An excellent edible fungus. Frequent.
Fr 6–10; P, D, Wd, H; S.

GENERAL FEATURES

The large *Macrolepiota* species are typical parasols. They have whitish spores, a moveable ring on the stem, and a scaly cap. Many smaller species occur which are similar to true parasols in form but differ in features such as gill attachment, spore colour, cap surface, and in microscopic characters.

HABITATS

Disturbed, rich or alkaline soil – beside ditches, for example, or in ash and beech woods – provides ideal conditions for many smaller parasols. The large *Macrolepiota* species can be found in dunes, parks and gardens. Golden cap will occur in similar places, often amongst nettles, whilst saffron parasol and its relatives occur in mossy places, usually on acid soil.

One interesting feature of the parasol and some of its relatives is the thick, double ring which forms a collar on the stem. This ring is loosely attached and can, with care, be moved up and down.

SHAGGY PARASOL
Macrolepiota rhacodes
H 10–20cm, CW 8–15cm, SW 1–2cm (base to 4cm). Cap scaly, stem smooth with double ring; flesh bruising pinkish. Common. Fr 6–11; P, Wd, H; S.

STINKING PARASOL
Lepiota cristata
H 3–5cm, CW 1–4cm, SW 2–4mm. Cap with small scales; centre slightly raised, orange-brown; stem with fragile ring; smell strong, unpleasant. Common. Fr 7–11; Wd, P, PE; S.

SOOTY PARASOL
Melanophyllum echinatum
H 2–5cm, CW 1–4cm, SW 1–3mm. Cap surface earth-coloured; young gills blood red. Spore deposit grey-green becoming red-brown. Occasional. Fr 6–11; P, Wd, H, W; S.

SAFFRON PARASOL
Cystoderma amianthinum
H 3–6cm, CW 2–4cm, SW 3–6mm. Cap yellow-brown with powdery surface and scales at edge; stem scaly below ring. Common. Fr 7–12; Wd, H; M, S.

GOLDEN CAP
Phaeolepiota aurea
H 10–20cm, CW 10–20cm, SW 15–35mm. Yellow-brown and mealy throughout; spores brown. Rare. Fr 7–10; P, Wd, H; S.

TRUE MUSHROOMS

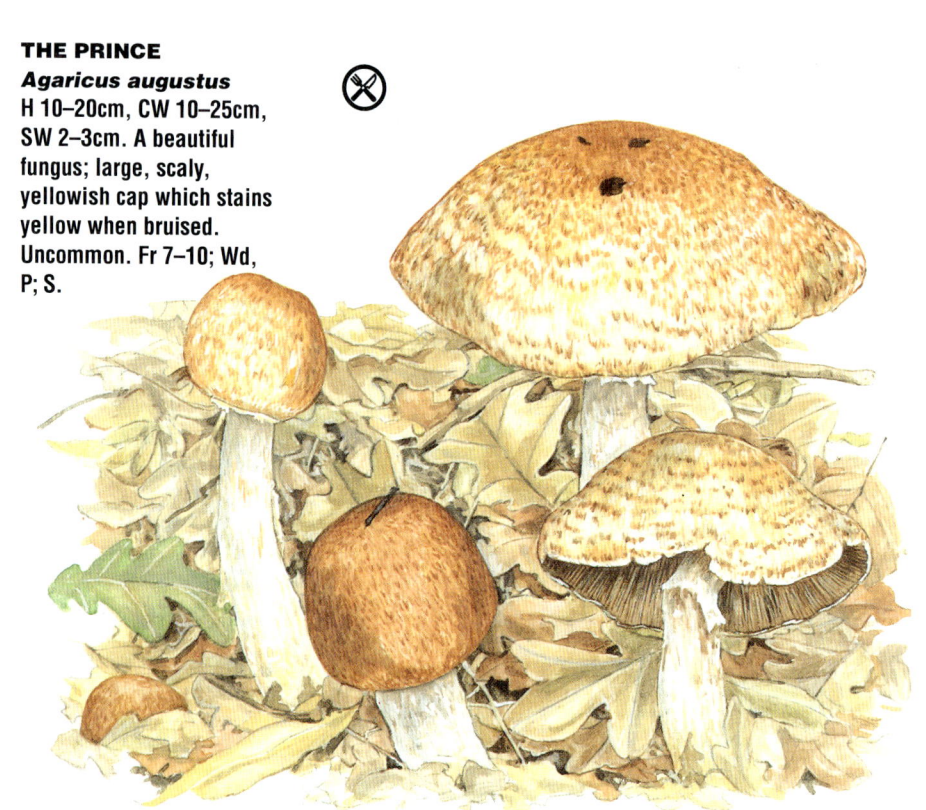

THE PRINCE
Agaricus augustus
H 10–20cm, CW 10–25cm, SW 2–3cm. A beautiful fungus; large, scaly, yellowish cap which stains yellow when bruised. Uncommon. Fr 7–10; Wd, P; S.

GENERAL FEATURES

Chocolate-brown spores, free gills and a ring on the stem are the main characteristics of these fungi, which all belong to the genus *Agaricus*. Some species have a pleasant smell like almond or aniseed, but a few, poisonous species have an unpleasant, inky smell.

HABITATS

Most of these species are found in rich or limey soil. Many occur in grassland or dunes, but others are found amongst leaf and needle litter in woods. Pavement mushroom (*A. bitorquis*) is well known for its habit of pushing up paving stones and asphalt.

The yellow stainer and its relatives are poisonous, and are best identified by cutting through the stem at the base. The flesh there will turn bright yellow immediately.

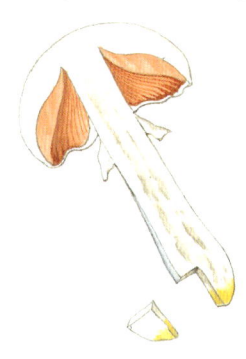

PROJECT

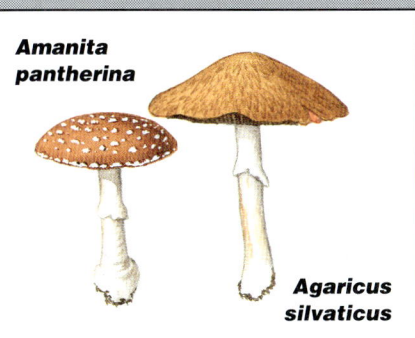

Amanita pantherina

Agaricus silvaticus

It is important to be able to distinguish between species of *Amanita* and *Agaricus*, since a mistake could prove fatal! Find different species belonging to the two groups and make a table listing features observed, such as colour of spore deposit and young gills, and presence and type of veils.

SCALY WOOD MUSHROOM
Agaricus silvaticus
H 5–10cm, CW 5–10cm, SW 10–15mm. Cap with brown, fibrous scales; stem swollen at base. Frequent. Fr 9–11; CWd, P; S, L.

FIELD MUSHROOM
Agaricus campestris
H 3–6cm, CW 3–10cm, SW 10–15mm. Cap fibrous-scaly, whitish, becoming pinkish; gills pink when young; stem thinner at base. Frequent. Fr 7–10; M, G, P, Md; S.

YELLOW STAINER
Agaricus xanthodermus
H 7–14cm, CW 5–12cm, SW 1–2cm. Cap greyish white, smooth or cracking; stem swollen at base; flesh yellowing strongly when cut, especially at base. Frequent. Fr 6–11; Wd, P, G; S.

HORSE MUSHROOM
Agaricus arvensis
H 6–12cm, CW 8–15cm, SW 1–3cm. A large, sturdy, whitish species with a well-developed cog-wheel on the ring underside. Surface stains yellow. Common. Fr 7–11; M, P, G, H; S.

101

SHIELD-CAPS AND VOLVARS

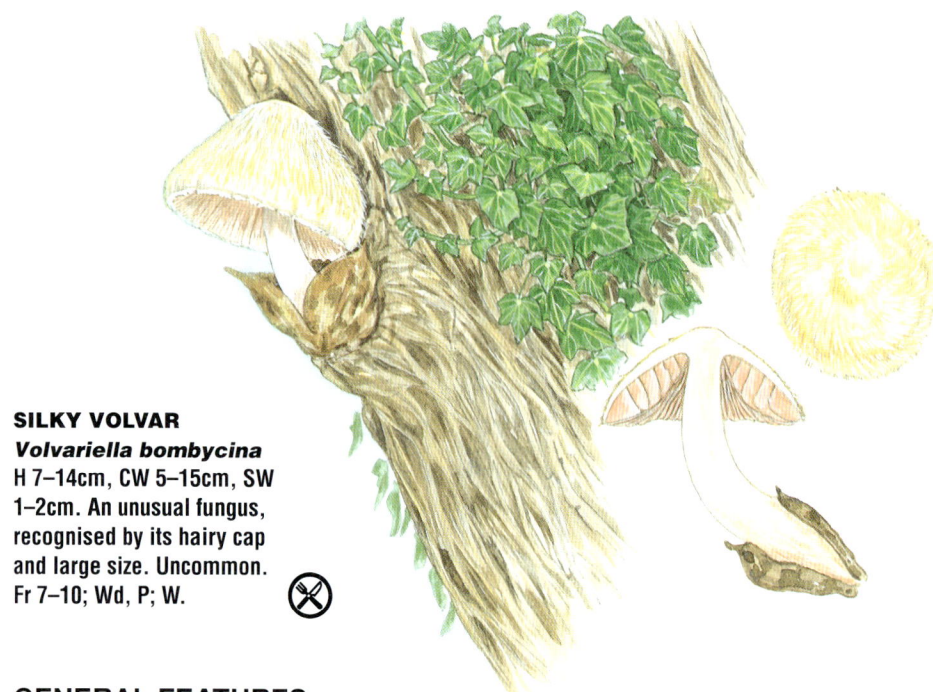

SILKY VOLVAR
Volvariella bombycina
H 7–14cm, CW 5–15cm, SW 1–2cm. An unusual fungus, recognised by its hairy cap and large size. Uncommon.
Fr 7–10; Wd, P; W.

GENERAL FEATURES

Shield-caps and volvars are mostly fleshy fungi which rot quickly. They have pink spores and crowded, free gills. The young fruitbodies of volvars are enclosed by a membrane which is later left as a bag or volva around the stem base. There is no ring on the stem of volvars or shield-caps. Some species are brightly coloured, but most are various shades of grey or brown. A few have a silky-fibrous cap, and some have small scales on the stem.

HABITATS

Most shield-caps grow on rotten wood of deciduous trees, although a few occur on conifer wood or on soil. Volvars are found in various habitats. The large silky volvar grows on wood, although other species are found in grass and on compost.

Large, fallen trunks in woodland are home to many insects and fungi, including most of the rarer shield-caps such as *Pluteus leoninus*. It is therefore important for managers of woodland to leave some decaying wood where it falls.

◁ **FAWN SHIELD-CAP**
Pluteus cervinus
H 6–12cm, CW 3–12cm, SW 5–15mm. Cap very dark brown at first, paler with age; gills white, then pink as spores mature. Common.
Fr 5–11; Wd, P, H; W.

YELLOW-FOOTED ▷
SHIELD-CAP
Pluteus romellii
H 3–6cm, CW 2–5cm, SW 3–6mm. Brownish, rather wrinkled cap, yellow stem; gills yellowish at first, then pink. Occasional to frequent.
Fr 6–11; DWd, P; W.

◁ **SLIMY VOLVAR**
Volvariella gloiocephala
H 8–16cm, CW 5–10cm, SW 5–15mm. Cap greyish or cream, slimy in wet weather, egg-shaped at first. Frequent, often on compost. Also known as *V. speciosa*.
Fr 6–11; P, G; S.

PARASITIC VOLVAR ▷
Volvariella surrecta
H 2–4cm, CW 3–5cm, SW 4–10mm. An unmistakeable white volvar, easily recognised by its habitat on rotting clouded agarics. Rare. Fr 9–11.

MILLERS AND PINK-GILLS

THE MILLER
Clitopilus prunulus
H 2–6cm, CW 3–10cm, SW 4–10mm. Cap whitish, domed then funnel-shaped, with wavy edge. Frequent. Fr 7–10; Wd, P; S.

GENERAL FEATURES

Millers are close relatives of pink-gills, but differ on microscopic characteristics. They have pale, whitish fruitbodies and smell strongly of fresh flour. Pink-gills vary greatly in size, shape and colour, but they all have pink spores.

HABITATS

Millers grow on soil or litter, both in woods and in grassy places. Pink-gills can be found in many habitats. The group known as blue-caps occurs mainly in alkaline grassland, whereas the larger, fleshy pink-gills usually grow under trees in woods or parks.

Few pink-gills grow on wood, but one of the most beautiful and interesting species – *Entoloma euchroum* – does so. This fungus is sometimes known as the violet pink-gill, and is found mainly on dead wood in alder carrs.

SILKY PINK-GILL
Entoloma sericeum
H 2–4cm, CW 2–5cm, SW 4–6mm. Cap dark brown, drying paler, with silky-streaky surface. Common. Fr 7–11; Md, G, P; S.

ROMAN SHIELD
Entoloma clypeatum
H 5–10cm, CW 3–10cm, SW 5–15mm. Cap grey-brown; strong, floury smell. Frequent. Fr 4–6; P, H; S.

SAW-GILLED BLUE-CAP
Entoloma serrulatum
H 3–6cm, CW 1.5–4cm, SW 2–3mm. Cap and stem blue-black; gills pinkish with saw-like blue-black or dark edge. Frequent. Fr 7–10; Md, P; S.

NITROUS PINK-GILL
Entoloma nidorosum
H 4–8cm, CW 2–5cm, SW 3–8mm. Cap pale brown, with striate edge. Stem paler. Frequent. Fr 8–11; DWd; S.

HOW TO FIND

Go out in spring when hawthorn is in flower. Find some of these trees, which are often planted in hedgerows, and look for roman shield (*Entoloma clypeatum*) growing under them. Later in the summer, visit a local meadow and look for the smaller, often brightly coloured pink-gills known as blue-caps (shown here). They will only be found if there has been rain recently.

BRITTLE-HEADS AND ALLIES

GENERAL FEATURES

These all have blackish or brown spores, and most have a veil. In some species this may leave fibres or a ring on the stem, which often looks black from fallen spores. Weeping widow, which belongs in the genus *Lacrymaria*, is notable for producing droplets on the gills. Brittle-heads, species of *Psathyrella*, are fragile and easily broken. They may grow singly or in tufts.

HABITATS

These fungi are found most often in disturbed or man-made habitats such as grass verges and compost heaps. However, there are also some true grassland species, and a few which grow on decaying wood. Even dung, fire sites and swamps support a few brittle-heads.

Some common brittle-heads are notable for having the edges of their gills lined with red. This is easy to see using a hand-lens. It is a character which is found in some bonnet-caps, but is not present in other dark-spored toadstools.

WEEPING WIDOW
Lacrymaria velutina
H 5–10cm, CW 3–10cm, SW 3–10mm. Yellow-brown, woolly-fibrous cap with fringed edge; black spores and weeping gills. Common. Fr 6–11; G, P, PE; S.

MARRAM BRITTLE-HEAD
Psathyrella ammophila
H 3–6cm, CW 2–5cm, SW 3–5mm. Cap brownish; stem growing from marram stems. Common. Fr 8–12; D; S.

WHITE BRITTLE-HEAD
Psathyrella candolleana
H 4–10cm, CW 2–7cm, SW 3–8mm. Cap whitish or pale brown, with tooth-like remains of veil at edge. Common. Fr 5–11; Wd, P, H; W, S.

TUFTED BRITTLE-HEAD
Psathyrella multipedata
H 6–12cm, CW 1.5–3cm, SW 2–4mm. Grows in large tufts. Cap grey-brown; stems rooting, whitish. Occasional. Fr 7–11; G, P; S.

COMMON STUMP BRITTLE-HEAD
Psathyrella piluliformis
H 5–10cm, CW 2–5cm, SW 3–7mm. Cap brown; stem silky white. Very common. Fr 8–12; DWd, P; W.

HOW TO FIND

Any foray in October will produce a number of brittle-heads. Most are difficult to name, as there are so many species. One of the easier ones is common stump brittle-head (shown here), which grows in clusters on rotten wood. It has rather pale gills and a white stem, and has a veil which leaves web-like remains at the edge of the cap.

INK-CAPS

SHAGGY INK-CAP
Coprinus comatus
H 12–35cm, SW 5–15mm.
Cap tall and cylinder-shaped,
5–15cm high. Also known as
lawyer's wig. Common.
Fr 7–10; P, PE, G, W; S.

GENERAL FEATURES

Ink-caps are black-spored fungi which have closely-spaced gills and, very often, a grooved cap. Most species have gills which break down into an inky fluid when the fungus is mature – hence the common name of this group. A veil is present in most species and can appear as scales, fibres or granules on the cap surface. The veil sometimes leaves a ring on the stem.

Common ink-cap (*Coprinus atramentarius*) is the main source of what is known as coprinus ink. This is made from the inky fluid which is produced as the fungus matures, and has been used for drawing and writing, and in photography.

HABITATS

All ink-caps are saprobes (see pp.8–9), living on decaying organic matter. They can be found on soil in woods or fields, on rotten wood, dung and manure, on burnt ground and in leaf and stem litter. Some species even occur in houses, on old, damp plaster and in cellars. Many small species occur on dung.

SHAGGY BONFIRE INK-CAP
Coprinus lagopides
H 5–14cm, CW 2–4cm, SW 3–10mm. Cap cylinder-shaped at first, shaggy from white veil. Stem white, also shaggy. Frequent. Fr 6–11; B.

SNOW-WHITE INK-CAP
Coprinus niveus
H 3–9cm, SW 3–6mm, cap 1–3cm high. Whole fruitbody pure white and mealy all over. Frequent, especially on horse dung. Fr 7–11; Dg.

GLISTENING INK-CAP
Coprinus micaceus
H 4–10cm, CW 2–4cm, SW 2–5mm. Cap yellow-brown, striate, covered in glistening granules which later disappear. Very common, growing in tufts. Fr 5–11; Wd, P, H; W.

DUNG INK-CAP
Coprinus miser
H 5–40mm, CW 2–8mm, SW 0.5mm. Cap reddish-brown, striate, smooth. Frequent, especially on cow and horse dung. Fr 1–12; Dg.

CONE-CAPS AND ALLIES

GENERAL FEATURES
These fungi vary greatly in form and colour, although their microscopic characteristics are very similar. They have brown or yellow-brown spores and a smooth cap surface. Species of *Bolbitius* are slimy and thin-fleshed. Cone-caps are mostly slender fungi, with cone-shaped, yellowish-brown caps, whilst field-caps are larger and more fleshy, and usually fruit in the springtime.

HABITATS
All cone-caps and related species are saprobes (see pp.8–9). Many species thrive on bare soil or in grass, while others are found on manure, compost and dung. Only a few species grow on rotten wood.

Most of the species in this group are inedible and some are poisonous. However, a few species, such as *Agrocybe cylindrica*, are good edible fungi and are grown especially for sale in some shops and markets.

YELLOW COW-PAT TOADSTOOL
Bolbitius vitellinus
H 4–9cm, CW 1–5cm, SW 2–4mm. Cap slimy, bright yellow, thin-fleshed and striate. Stem paler, with mealy surface. Common.
Fr 5–11; Md, G, P; S.

PROJECT

The yellow cow-pat toadstool grows amongst rotten grass and on manure. It has thin flesh and quickly shrivels, rather like an ink-cap. Find some specimens of this fungus and an ink-cap such as glistening ink-cap and compare how their fruitbodies develop with age.

MILKY CONE-CAP ▽
Conocybe lactea
H 5–10cm, CW 1–2cm, SW 1–3mm. Cap thimble-shaped, whitish, stem fragile. Occasional.
Fr 6–10; G, P; S.

BULB-FOOT CONE-CAP ▽
Conocybe subovalis
H 6–10cm, CW 2–4cm, SW 1–2mm, 3–4mm at base. Cap dull yellow-brown, striate when fresh. Stem slender, with swollen base. Frequent.
Fr 8–10; G, P, PE; S.

SPRING FIELD-CAP ▲
Agrocybe praecox
H 4–8cm, CW 3–7cm, SW 4–8mm. Cap yellowish-brown. Stem with ring and swollen base. Smell floury. Frequent. Fr 5–6, 10–12; P, PE, G, Wd; S, Ma.

PALE FIELD-CAP ▲
Agrocybe dura
H 5–10cm, CW 3–8cm, SW 3–8mm. Cap pale, creamy-yellow and often cracking. Veil remains on cap edge. Occasional. Fr 5–7; G, P, S.

SLIME-CAPS AND ALLIES

BLUE-GREEN SLIME-CAP
Stropharia cyanea
H 3–10cm, CW 2–6cm, SW 4–8mm. Blue-green throughout when fresh. Veil leaves white, cottony teeth at cap edge. Stem cottony, without a ring. Common.
Fr 8–11; DWd, P, PE; S, Ma.

GENERAL FEATURES

These fungi generally have purple-black or black spores. Slime-caps, some of which are brightly coloured, may be very slimy, and they all have a ring on the stem. The closely-related liberty-caps are usually smaller, less slimy, and with duller colours. Mottle-gills are so-called because the sides of their gills are mottled by clumps of spores (best viewed with a hand-lens).

HABITATS

All of these fungi are saprobes (see pp.8–9). Many occur in grassy places or in parks, others are found on dung or manure. Wood-chips put onto flowerbeds and paths are also an increasingly important habitat for these fungi.

One of the most attractive of the slime-caps is orange slime-cap, *Stropharia aurantiaca*. This species can grow happily on the wood-chips that are now spread on flowerbeds and paths in gardens. Once very rare, it is now spreading rapidly as a result of this practice.

FRINGED HAY-CAP
Panaeolus sphinctrinus
H 6–12cm, CW 1–4cm, SW 2–3mm. Cap grey-brown, with characteristic fringed, white edge. Stem with mealy surface. Common. Fr 5–10; G, Md; Dg, Ma.

LIBERTY CAP
Psilocybe semilanceata
H 4–8cm, CW 5–15mm, SW 1–2mm. Cap olive-grey, drying yellowish, striate when fresh. Stem sometimes blue at base. Frequent. Fr 8–11; G, Md, P; S.

SHINY HAY-CAP
Panaeolus semiovatus
H 6–12cm, CW 2–4cm, SW 2–6mm. Cap oval, smooth, sticky when wet, pale; stem with fragile ring. Common. Fr 4–12; Md, G; Dg.

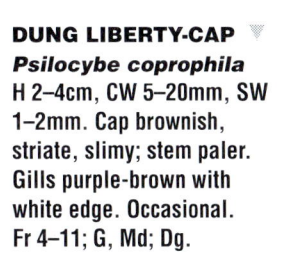

DUNG LIBERTY-CAP
Psilocybe coprophila
H 2–4cm, CW 5–20mm, SW 1–2mm. Cap brownish, striate, slimy; stem paler. Gills purple-brown with white edge. Occasional. Fr 4–11; G, Md; Dg.

HAY-CAP
Panaeolus foenisecii
H 4–8cm, CW 1–2.5cm, SW 2–3mm. Cap bell-shaped when young, dark brown; becomes paler from centre, leaving darker zone at edge. Gills brown. Very common. Fr 6–10; P, G; S.

SCALE-HEADS & SULPHUR-CAPS

SHAGGY SCALE-HEAD
Pholiota squarrosa
H 5–12cm, CW 4–12cm, SW 10–20mm. Cap and stem yellowish, dry, covered with coarse, curved scales. Common. Fr 9–11; DWd, P; W.

GENERAL FEATURES

Species of *Pholiota* are popularly known as scale-heads because many of them have obvious scales. They all have brown spores and many are bright yellow in colour, but they vary in other characteristics. Sulphur-caps, too, are often yellow, but their spores are purple-brown and they never have prominent scales. However, they have a veil which may leave web-like remains near the cap edge. Some of these fungi grow in tufts, but others grow singly.

Poplar scale-head, *Pholiota destruens*, is a very large and distinctive, but uncommon, species. It is a parasite that grows on poplar trees, eventually destroying its host.

HABITATS

Although most scale-heads are saprobes (see pp.8–9), often occurring on rotten wood or litter, a few species are parasitic. One species is common on burnt ground. Sulphur-caps are not parasites, and can be found in various habitats. Several species grow on wood, although the smaller species are found mainly amongst moss.

SULPHUR TUFT
Hypholoma fasciculare
H 5–10cm, CW 2–5cm, SW 3–6mm. Cap yellow, reddish at centre when young. Gills greenish then purple-black. Very common. Fr 5–11; Wd, P; W.

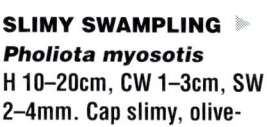

SLIMY SWAMPLING
Pholiota myosotis
H 10–20cm, CW 1–3cm, SW 2–4mm. Cap slimy, olive-brown, with whitish veil remains at edge. Stem rooting deep in moss. Gill edge white. Frequent. Fr 8–10; M; M.

BRICK CAP
Hypholoma sublateritium
H 6–12cm, CW 3–10cm, SW 5–12mm. Cap brick red with whitish veil at edge. Gills pale yellowish, later purple-grey. Frequent, in tufts. Fr 8–11; DWd, P; W.

CHARCOAL SCALE-HEAD
Pholiota carbonaria
H 3–7cm, CW 2–5cm, SW 3–8mm. Cap reddish-brown, slimy in wet weather. Stem with cottony fibres and ring zone. Gills olive-brown. Frequent. Fr 6–11; B.

FIBRE-CAPS AND FAIRY-CAKES

COMMON WHITE FIBRE-CAP
Inocybe geophylla
H 3–6cm, CW 1–4cm, SW 2–5mm. Cap cone-shaped, later expanding, with raised centre; white or lilac. Stem with floury surface and fibrous veil remains. Common. Fr 6–11; Wd, P; S.

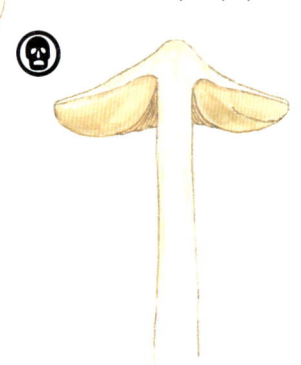

GENERAL FEATURES

These fungi have clay-brown spores, and are mostly brown-coloured species. Fibre-caps have smooth or felty to scaly caps which always have fibres arranged in a radial pattern, like the spokes of a wheel. Some have a swollen stem base. Some fairy-cakes have weeping gills, others have a well-developed veil. They have smooth caps which are more deeply coloured towards the centre. Brownies are small and dull-coloured, and so are easily overlooked.

HABITATS

Fibre-caps and fairy-cakes are usually mycorrhizal (see pp.8–9), and most are woodland fungi. However, some occur in more open habitats with willow and birch. A few fairy-cakes occur on burnt ground or in other habitats. Brownies are found on decaying wood, leaf litter and soil.

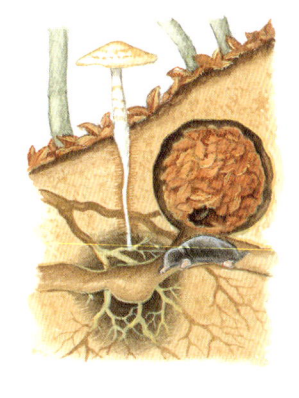

The rooting fairy-cake has an especially interesting life history. It has been shown that it always grows from the toilet sites of moles, which are found underground near to their nests. The species is widespread throughout Britain and northern Europe.

COMMON BROWN FIBRE-CAP
Inocybe lacera
H 2–5cm, CW 2–4cm, SW 2–5mm. Cap and stem brown, felty-fibrous all over. Gills grey-brown with white edge. Common, on sandy soil. Fr 6–10; Wd, P, D; S.

WEEPING FAIRY-CAKE
Hebeloma crustuliniforme
H 4–8cm, CW 4–8cm, SW 5–15mm. Cap pale buff; stem whitish. Gills weeping. Smells of radishes. Also known as poison pie. Common. Fr 8–11; Wd, P; S.

COMMON VEILED FAIRY-CAKE
Hebeloma mesophaeum
H 3–7cm, CW 2–5cm, SW 3–6mm. Cap reddish-brown at centre, edge paler and with web-like veil remains. Stem with brownish base and veil fibres near top. Common. Fr 8–11; CWd, P, B; S.

ROOTING FAIRY-CAKE
Hebeloma radicosum
H 5–10cm, CW 5–10cm, SW 10–15mm. Cap pale yellow-brown, edge woolly from veil; stem scaly below the ring, deep rooting. Smell marzipan-like. Occasional. Fr 8–10; DWd; S.

COMMON BROWNIE
Tubaria furfuracea
H 2–5cm, CW 1–3cm, SW 2–3mm. Cap pale reddish-brown, finely striate when fresh, with whitish scales near edge. Stem with fine, silky fibres. Common. Fr 1–12; Wd, P, H, W; L.

WEB-CAPS

RED-BANDED WEB-CAP
Cortinarius armillatus
H 6–12cm, CW 5–12cm, SW 1–3cm. Cap red-brown with small scales. Stem paler, with several reddish bands. Occasional, with birch.
Fr 8–10; DWd; S.

GENERAL FEATURES

Web-caps have rusty-brown spores and a web-like veil which is known as a cortina – hence their genus name, *Cortinarius*. The cortina may leave various white or coloured bands on the stem. Web-caps are very variable. A few are brightly coloured, although most are a dull brown, and some are slimy whilst others are completely dry.

One group of bright-coloured web-caps, sometimes called *Dermocybe*, are ideal for use in dyeing wool. This can then be used for making sweaters and other garments.

HABITATS

These fungi are considered to be mycorrhizal (see pp.8–9), and are thus most common in woodlands. Different species are found with coniferous (evergreen) and deciduous (leaf-shedding) trees. Some species are restricted to bogs, and others occur only in dunes.

BLUE-BANDED WEB-CAP
Cortinarius collinitus
H 6–12cm, CW 4–8cm, SW 5–15mm. Cap orange-brown, slimy; stem with slimy, violet covering, becoming banded. Occasional to frequent. Fr 8–10; CWd; S.

PURPLISH WEB-CAP
Cortinarius purpurascens
H 5–10cm, CW 5–12cm, SW 1–2.5cm, wider at base. Cap sticky when wet, grey-brown to chestnut; stem, gills and flesh purplish. Frequent. Fr 8–10; Wd; S.

PELARGONIUM WEB-CAP
Cortinarius paleaceus
H 3–7cm, CW 1–3cm, SW 2–5mm. Cap dark brown, covered in silky scales. Smells like geranium plants. Frequent. Fr 8–10; DWd, M; S, M.

ORANGE BOG WEB-CAP
Cortinarius uliginosus
H 3–6cm, CW 2–5cm, SW 3–8mm. Cap coppery-orange, dry. Yellowish veil fibres at edge of cap and on stem. Stem paler; flesh yellow. Gills bright yellow at first. Occasional, with willow. Fr 8–10; M; S.

PIXY-CAPS AND FLAME-CAPS

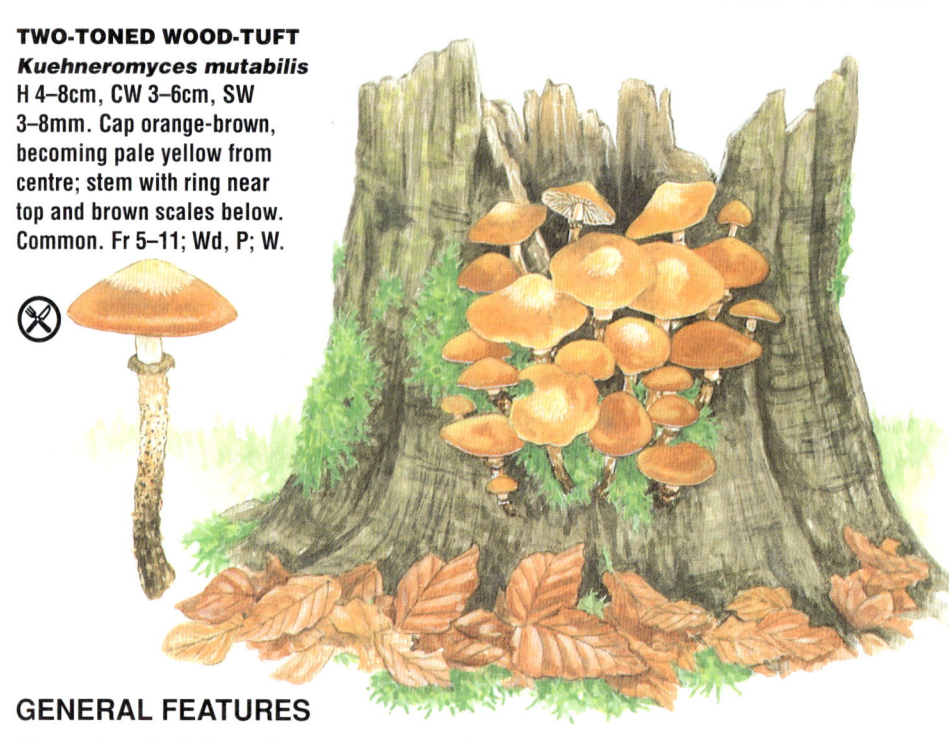

TWO-TONED WOOD-TUFT
Kuehneromyces mutabilis
H 4–8cm, CW 3–6cm, SW 3–8mm. Cap orange-brown, becoming pale yellow from centre; stem with ring near top and brown scales below. Common. Fr 5–11; Wd, P; W.

GENERAL FEATURES

These fungi all have brown or rusty-brown spores, and fruitbodies which are orange, brown or yellow in colour. Pixy-caps are mostly small and slender, and sometimes have a veil which leaves a ring-like zone on the stem. Flame-caps are bright orange or yellow. They belong to the small genus *Gymnopilus*, and are identified mostly by microscopic characteristics. Two-toned wood-tuft belongs in a different group. It has a scaly stem with an obvious ring.

The poisonous *Galerina marginata* (the two toadstools on the right in the photograph) and some of its close relatives are similar to two-toned wood-tuft (left) and also grow on wood. They differ mainly in lacking scales on the stem.

HABITATS

Flame-caps are mostly found on decaying wood, usually growing singly or occasionally in tufts. Some pixy-caps also thrive on rotten wood, although most grow amongst moss or grass. Two-toned wood-tuft grows in large tufts and clusters on rotten logs and stumps.

GIANT FLAME-CAP
Gymnopilus junonius
H 6–12cm, CW 5–15cm, SW 5–15mm. Cap orange-yellow, streaky; stem paler, with ring. In tufts at base of trees. Frequent. Fr 8–10; Wd, P; W.

FRECKLED FLAME-CAP
Gymnopilus penetrans
H 3–6cm, CW 2–6cm, SW 3–8mm. Cap rusty-yellow; gills yellow with rusty spots. Common. Fr 8–11; Wd; W.

PROJECT

As with many toadstools, the cap of two-toned wood-tuft (shown here) becomes paler from the centre as it dries. The process also works in reverse – dry caps become darker in wet conditions. You can test this yourself, using a range of fungi of different species, including two-toned wood-tuft. Place the stem through a hole in a sheet of paper and into a glass of water. Cover it with a large glass jar, and observe the colour change.

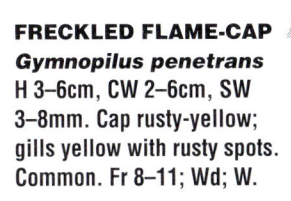

BOG PIXY-CAP
Galerina tibiicystis
H 5–12cm, CW 1–3cm, SW 2–3mm. Cap orange-yellow, drying paler, without a veil. Frequent, in *Sphagnum* moss. Fr 5–9; M; M.

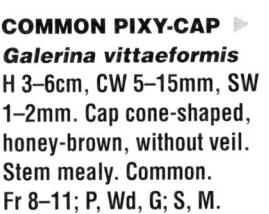

COMMON PIXY-CAP
Galerina vittaeformis
H 3–6cm, CW 5–15mm, SW 1–2mm. Cap cone-shaped, honey-brown, without veil. Stem mealy. Common. Fr 8–11; P, Wd, G; S, M.

RUSSULES

YELLOW SWAMP RUSSULE
Russula claroflava
H 5–10cm, CW 5–10cm, SW 1–2cm. Bright yellow cap and paler gills. Spores pale yellow. Frequent, on damp ground under birch. Fr 7–10; DWd, M; S.

GENERAL FEATURES

A large group, with over 120 species in northwest Europe, russules are easily recognised by their bright-coloured caps, white stems and brittle flesh. Their spores range in colour from white to yellow-orange, depending on the species. Some have a characteristic smell. Russules are close relatives of the milk-caps, but lack the milky fluid.

A few of the larger, blackening russules often have fungi growing on them. These are parasitic toadstools of the genus *Asterophora*.

HABITATS

Species of *Russula* grow in mycorrhizal association (see pp.8–9) with trees, and are mostly woodland fungi. A few grow with creeping willow and are found in dunes. Ancient parkland, with old, scattered trees, can support many russules, including rare species that are no longer found elsewhere.

PROJECT

Find as many different species of *Russula* as possible on a day's foray. Woodlands and old parkland are the best places to look. Take the specimens home, and use one of each to prepare spore deposits (leave them overnight with the caps laid onto a sheet of white paper). Compare the deposits and note the differences in colour.

THE SICKENER
Russula emetica
H 5–10cm, CW 4–10cm, SW 1–2cm. Striking, bright red cap; white stem and gills. Spores white. Very common. Fr 6–10; Wd; S.

PURPLE-BLACK RUSSULE
Russula atropurpurea
H 3–6cm, CW 4–10cm, SW 1–2cm. Cap purple-red, with dark centre; gills white. Spores white. Common, especially with oak. Fr 7–10; Wd; S.

THE CHARCOAL BURNER
Russula cyanoxantha
H 5–10cm, CW 5–12cm, SW 1–3cm. Cap usually lilac or greenish. Gills whitish, spores white. Common. Fr 6–10; DWd; S.

BLACKENING RUSSULE
Russula nigricans
H 4–9cm, CW 5–20cm, SW 1–3cm. Large, brown cap. Flesh bruises red then black. Spores white. Common. Fr 7–10; Wd; S.

MILK-CAPS

GENERAL FEATURES

The most obvious feature of milk-caps is the milky fluid that is present in the flesh. This is easily seen when the flesh or gills of fresh specimens are broken. In a few species, the milk is watery, and there is only a small quantity, but usually the milk is white and plentiful. However, in some milk-caps, the milk is a characteristic colour or changes colour as it dries. Most milk-caps are dull in colour.

HABITATS

Milk-caps are mycorrhizal (see pp.8–9) and usually restricted to one or a few tree species. Several of these fungi are adapted to wet habitats such as alder and willow carrs.

The milk of a milk-cap may change colour as it dries, and this can provide an important clue for identifying it. A white handkerchief is useful for testing possible colour changes – just press the handkerchief against the broken flesh to soak up some milk, and watch closely.

WOOLLY MILK-CAP
Lactarius torminosus
H 4–8cm, CW 4–12cm, SW 1–2cm. An attractive species; the pinkish, zoned cap has a characteristic woolly, rolled edge. Frequent, with birch.
Fr 7–10; DWd; S.

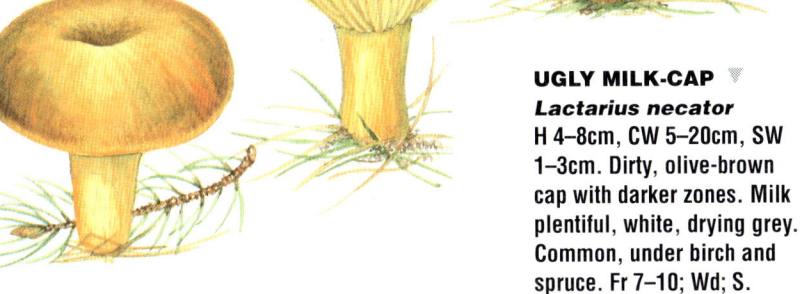

SPRUCE MILK-CAP
Lactarius deterrimus
H 5–10cm, CW 5–10cm, SW 1–2cm. Cap zoned, orange, becoming greenish. Milk carrot coloured, later green. Frequent, under young spruce. Fr 7–11; CWd; S.

UGLY MILK-CAP
Lactarius necator
H 4–8cm, CW 5–20cm, SW 1–3cm. Dirty, olive-brown cap with darker zones. Milk plentiful, white, drying grey. Common, under birch and spruce. Fr 7–10; Wd; S.

RUFOUS MILK-CAP
Lactarius rufus
H 4–8cm, CW 4–10cm, SW 5–15mm. Cap reddish-brown with raised centre. Milk white. Common, under spruce, pine and birch. Fr 6–11; Wd; S.

ALDER MILK-CAP
Lactarius obscuratus
H 2–4cm, CW 1–3cm, SW 3–5mm. Cap striate at edge, with small, olive-coloured hump at centre. Milk white. Frequent, with alder. Fr 5–10; Wd, M; S.

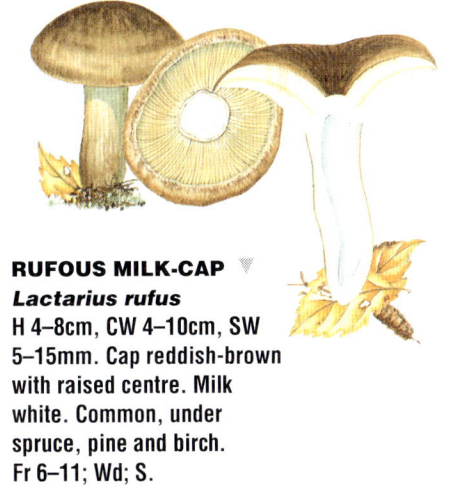

INDEX

A
Agaricus, 22, 100, 101
Agaricus arvensis, 23, 101
Agaricus augustus, 100
Agaricus bisporus, 17
Agaricus bitorquis, 100
Agaricus campestris, 26, 101
Agaricus silvaticus, 34, 101
Agaricus xanthodermus, 101
Agrocybe cylindrica, 110
Agrocybe dura, 111
Agrocybe praecox, 111
Alder bracket, 25, 63
Alder milk-cap, 25, 125
Aleuria aurantia, 23, 43
Amanita, 13, 96, 101
Amanita fulva, 97
Amanita muscaria, 4, 39, 96
Amanita pantherina, 100
Amanita phalloides, 97
Amanita rubescens, 97
Amanita virosa, 97
Anthracobia maurilabra, 28, 47
Armillaria ectypa, 19
Armillaria mellea, 84
Artist's fungus, 36, 58
asci, 5, 42, 48, 50
Ascobolus furfuraceus, 30, 47
Asterophora, 122
Aurantiporus croceus, 19
Auricularia auricula-judae, 52, 53
Auriscalpium vulgare, 33, 71

B
basidium, 5, 52
Beech jelly-disc, 36, 49
Beefsteak fungus, 38, 64
Birch polypore, 39, 60
bird's-nest fungi, 54, 56
Bitter bracket, 35, 61
Black bonnet-cap, 29, 82
Blackening wax-cap, 26, 82
Blushing bracket, 24, 61
Bog pixy-cap, 25, 121
Bolbitius vitellinus, 26, 110
boletes, 74–7
Boletus chrysenteron, 75
Boletus edulis, 75
Boletus erythropus, 36, 74
Boletus parasiticus, 38, 75
Boletus regius, 19
Bonfire chanterelle, 28, 81
Bonfire navel-cap, 29, 87
Bovista nigrescens, 55
bracket fungi, 58–65
Brown dung-cup, 30

Brown hay-cap, 22, 113
Brown roll-rim, 39, 78
Bulgaria inquinans, 53

C
Calocera viscosa, 32, 53, 69
Calocybe gambosa, 95
Calvatia utriformis, 26, 55
Candle snuff fungus, 22, 50
Cantharellus cibarius, 33, 71
Cantharellus tubiformis, 71
Cauliflower fungus, 33, 69
Chanterelle, 33, 71
Charcoal burner, 36, 123
Charcoal scale-head, 29, 115
Chlorosplenium aeruginascens, 11
Ciboria batschiana, 11
Clavaria argillacea, 41, 67
Clavaria vermicularis, 67
Clavaria zollingeri, 66
Clavariadelphus pistillaris, 66
Claviceps purpurea, 21
Clavulina cristata, 67
Clavulinopsis corniculata, 27, 67, 69
Clitocybe clavipes, 85
Clitocybe odora, 85
Clitopilus prunulus, 104
Collybia butyracea, 93
Collybia confluens, 93
Collybia dryophila, 93
Collybia fusipes, 38, 92
Collybia maculata, 34, 93
Collybia peronata, 93
Collybia racemosa, 92
Common bonfire cup, 28, 47
Common brown fibre-cap, 40, 117
Common earthball, 38, 57
Common white saddle, 22, 42
Conocybe lactea, 111
Conocybe subovalis, 111
Coprinus atramentarius, 108
Coprinus comatus, 108
Coprinus lagopides, 28, 109
Coprinus micaceus, 109
Coprinus miser, 31, 109
Coprinus niveus, 30, 109
Coprobia granulata, 31, 47
Cordyceps ophioglossoides, 35, 51
Cortinarius armillatus, 118
Cortinarius collinitus, 119
Cortinarius paleaceus, 119
Cortinarius purpurascens, 119
Cortinarius uliginosus, 25, 119
Cramp balls, 37, 51
Craterellus cornucopioides, 37, 71

cup fungi, 4, 42–49
Cyathus olla, 23, 57
Cystoderma amianthinum, 99

D
Dacrymyces stillatus, 53
Dacrymycetales, 6
Daldinia concentrica, 37, 51
Daedaleopsis confragosa, 24, 61
Dermocybe, 118
Dotted-stem bolete, 36, 74
Dune cup, 41, 45
Dune earth-tongue, 41, 49
Dune stinkhorn, 41
Dune wax-cap, 41, 83
Dung ink-cap, 31, 109
Dung liberty-cap, 30, 113
Dung orange-spot, 31, 47
Dwarf earth-star, 41, 55

E
Ear pick-fungus, 33, 71
earthballs, 56
earth-stars, 54
Elaphomyces granulatus, 35, 51
Entoloma clypeatum, 105
Entoloma euchroum, 104
Entoloma madidum, 19
Entoloma nidorosum, 105
Entoloma sericeum, 105
Entoloma serrulatum, 105
ergots, 21
Exidia glandulosa, 53

F
Faerberia carbonaria, 28, 81
Fairy ring champignon, 22, 90
False chanterelle, 32, 79
Field mushroom, 26, 101
Fistulina hepatica, 38, 64
Flamulina velutipes, 93
Fly agaric, 39, 96
Fomes fomentarius, 59
Fomitopsis pinicola, 34, 59
Freckled flame-cap, 33, 121
Fringed hay-cap, 31, 113
Fuligo septica, 73

G
Galerina marginata, 120
Galerina tibiicystis, 25, 121
Galerina vittaeformis, 121
Ganoderma applanatum, 36, 58
Ganoderma lucidum, 21
Geastrum nanum, 41, 55
Geoglossum arenarium, 41, 49

Geoglossum fallax, 27, 49
Geopyxis carbonaria, 28, 45
Gomphales, 7
Gomphidius glutinosus, 79
Gomphidius roseus, 79
Gymnopilus, 120
Gymnopilus junonius, 121
Gymnopilus penetrans, 33, 121
Gyromitra, 42

H
Hart's truffle, 35, 51
Heath fairy-club, 41, 67
Heath navel-cap, 41, 87
Hebeloma crustuliniforme, 117
Hebeloma mesophaeum, 117
Hebeloma radicosum, 117
Hedgehog puffball, 37, 55
Helvella acetabula, 43
Helvella crispa, 22, 42
Helvella elastica, 43
Hericium clathroides, 19
Horn-of-plenty, 37, 71
Horse-hair fungus, 41, 91
Horse mushroom, 23, 101
Hydnellum, 70
Hydnum, 70
Hydnum repandum, 70
Hygrocybe conica, 26, 82
Hygrocybe conica var. *conicoides*, 41, 83
Hygrocybe nigrescens, 19
Hygrocybe pratensis, 27, 83
Hygrocybe psittacina, 27, 83
Hygrocybe russocoriaceus, 82
Hygrocybe virginea, 83
Hygrophoropsis aurantiacus, 32, 79
Hygrophorus agathosmus, 82
Hygrophorus cossus, 82
Hygrophorus hypothejus, 83
Hymenochaete, 64
Hymenochaete rubiginosa, 65
Hypoxylon frágiforme, 51
Hypholoma fasciculare, 115
Hypholoma sublateritium, 115

I
Inocybe geophylla, 116
Inocybe lacera, 40, 117
Inonotus radiatus, 25, 63

J
Jelly antler-fungus, 32, 53
Jelly baby, 24, 48

K
King Alfred's cakes, 37
Kuehneromyces mutabilis, 120

L
Lachnum virgineum, 49
Laccaria amethystea, 91
Laccaria laccata, 91
Lacrymaria, 106
Lacrymaria velutina, 106
Lactarius deterrimus, 35, 125
Lactarius necator, 125
Lactarius obscuratus, 25, 125
Lactarius rufus, 125
Lactarius torminosus, 124
Laetiporus sulphureus, 65
Langermannia gigantea, 54
Larch bolete, 34, 77
Laricifomes officinalis, 19
Leccinum, 76
Leccinum scabrum, 77
Leccinum versipelle, 39, 76
Leotia lubrica, 24, 48
Leotiales, 7
Lepiota, 36
Lepiota cristata, 37, 99
Lepista, 94
Lepista nuda, 23, 95
Leptosphaeria acuta, 51
Liberty cap, 27, 113
Lilac bonnet-cap, 36, 89
Little dung brush, 30
Lycoperdon echinatum, 37, 55

M
Macrolepiota, 98
Macrolepiota procera, 40, 98
Macrolepiota rhacodes, 23, 99
Marasmius, 90
Marasmius androsaceus, 41, 91
Marasmius oreades, 22, 90
Marasmius rotula, 91
Marram bonnet-cap, 40, 89
Marram brittle-head, 40, 107
Meadow coral-fungus, 27, 67
Meadow wax-cap, 27, 83
Megacollybia platyphylla, 85
Melanophyllum echinatum, 99
Mitrula paludosa, 49
Monilinia fructigena, 48
Morchella esculenta, 43
morels, 42
Mutinus caninus, 57
Mycena chlorantha, 40, 89
Mycena crocata, 88
Mycena haematopus, 88
Mycena inclinata, 38, 88
Mycena leucogala, 29, 89
Mycena pura, 36, 89
Mycena stylobates, 89
mycorrhizal fungi, 8, 22, 34, 36, 38, 56, 70, 74, 78, 82, 90, 94, 96, 116, 118, 122, 124

Myriostoma coliforme, 19
Myxomphalia maura, 29, 87

N
Neobulgaria pura, 36, 49

O
Oak bonnet-cap, 38, 89
Ochre-green coral-fungus, 35, 69
Octospora, 46
Omphalina ericetorum, 87
Omphalina pyxidata, 41, 87
Onygena equina, 73
Orange birch bolete, 39, 76
Orange bog web-cap, 25, 119
Orange peel fungus, 23, 43
Orange-zoned bracket, 34, 59
Otidea onotica, 43
Oudemansiella mucida, 37, 85

P
Paecilomyces farinosus, 73
Panaeolus foenisecii, 22, 113
Panaeolus semiovatus, 31, 113
Panaeolus sphinctrinus, 31, 113
Panellus serotinus, 81
parasites, 8, 9, 22, 24, 62, 84
Parasol mushroom, 40, 98
Parrot wax-cap, 27, 83
Paxillus atrotomentosus, 79
Paxillus involutus, 39, 78
Penicillium, 20, 73
Peziza ammophila, 41, 44, 45
Peziza arvernensis, 44
Peziza bovina, 30
Peziza micropus, 44
Peziza praetervisa, 28, 45
Peziza succosa, 45
Peziza vesiculosa, 44
Phaeolepiota aurea, 99
Phallus impudicus, 56
Pholiota, 114
Pholiota carbonaria, 29, 115
Pholiota destruens, 114
Pholiota myosotis, 24, 115
Pholiota squarrosa, 114
Phellinus igniarius, 63
Phellodon, 70
Pilobolus, 31, 72
Piptoporus, 60
Piptoporus betulinus, 39, 60
Pleurotus, 80
Pleurotus dryinus, 81
Pleurotus ostreatus, 80
Pleuteus cervinus, 103
Pleuteus leoninus, 102
Pleuteus romellii, 103
Plums-and-custard, 32, 94
poisonous fungi, 16
polypores, 7, 62

Polyporus squamosus, 62
Polyporus tuberaster, 62
Polyporus varius, 63
Porcelain fungus, 37, 85
Poronia punctata, 19
Psilocybe coprophila, 30, 113
Psilocybe semilanceata, 27, 113
Psathyrella, 106
Psathyrella ammophila, 40, 107
Psathyrella candolleana, 107
Psathyrella multipedata, 107
Psathyrella piluliformis, 107
Pseudotrametes gibbosa, 59
puffballs, 4, 54, 56
Purple-black russule, 38, 123
Purple bonfire cup, 28, 45
Pycnostysanus azaleae, 10

R
Ramaria, 68
Ramaria abietina, 35, 69
Ramaria decurrens, 68
Ramaria stricta, 68
Rickenella fibula, 86
Rickenella swartzii, 87
Russula, 36, 122, 123
Russula atropurpurea, 38, 123
Russula claroflava, 25, 122
Russula cyanoxantha, 36, 123
Russula emetica, 123
Russula nigricans, 123
rusts, 4, 8

S
Saccharomycotina, 6
saprobes, 8, 92, 94, 110, 112, 114
Sarcoscypha coccinea, 46

Sarcosoma globosum, 19
Scaly earth-tongue, 27, 49
Scaly meadow puffball, 26, 55
Scaly wood mushroom, 34, 101
Scleroderma citrinum, 38, 57
Scurfy dung-cup, 30, 47
Scutellinia scutellata, 47
Sepedonium chrysospermum, 74
Serpula lacrymans, 21
Shaggy bonfire ink-cap, 28, 109
Shaggy parasol, 23, 99
Shiny hay-cap, 31, 113
Shooting dung-fungus, 31, 72
Silky-grey knight-cap, 34, 95
Slender truffle-club, 35, 51
Slimy swampling, 24, 115
Slippery Jack, 33, 77
Snow-white ink-cap, 30, 108
Sparassis crispa, 33, 69
Sphaerobolus stellatus, 57
Sphagnum, 86, 92
Sphagnum greyling, 24, 93
Spindle shank, 38, 92
Spotted tough-shank, 34, 93
Spruce milk-cap, 35, 125
Stalked bonfire cup, 28, 45
Stereum, 64
Stereum hirsutum, 65
Stereum sanguinolentum, 65
Stinking parasol, 37, 99
stinkhorns, 54, 56
Strobilomyces strobilaceus, 77
Strobilurus, 33
Stropharia aurantiaca, 112
Stropharia cyanea, 112
Suillus bovinus, 78
Suillus grevillei, 34, 77
Suillus luteus, 33, 77

T
Tephrocybe palustris, 24, 93
Thelephora palmata, 69
Thelephora terrestris, 69
Torrendia pulchella, 19
Trametes, 60
Trametes versicolor, 61
Trichaptum, 60
Trichaptum abietinum, 32, 61
Tricholoma, 94
Tricholoma sulphureum, 95
Tricholoma virgatum, 34, 95
Tricholomopsis rutilans, 32, 94
Trumpet bird's-nest, 23, 57
Tubaria furfuracea, 117
Tuber aestivum, 50
Tylopilus felleus, 75
Tyromyces stipticus, 35, 61

V
Violet conifer bracket, 32, 61
Volvariella bombycina, 102
Volvariella gloiocephala, 103
Volvariella surrecta, 103

W
Wood blewit, 23, 95

X
Xylaria carpophila, 11
Xylaria hypoxylon, 22, 50

Y
Yellow cow-pat toadstool, 26, 110
Yellow swamp russule, 25, 122

ILLUSTRATIONS BY
(t = top, b = bottom, l = left, r = right, c = centre)

Ian Fleming Associates/ Catharine Slade 43, 47, 49, 59, 65, 71t, 71b, 75t, 75cr, 85, 95t, 97cl, 99tl, 99bl, 99br, 103, 125; Garden Studios/Andrew Beckett 22–23, 24–25, 26–27, 28–29, 30–31, 32–33, 34–35, 36–37, 38–39, 40–41 /Roger Kent 6–7, 17, 19, 45tl, 45tr, 45c, 45br, 51, 53, 55, 57, 61, 63, 67, 69, 73t, 73cl, 73bl, 73br, 79, 81tr, 81cr, 83tr, 83c, 87t, 87cr, 89, 91cl, 91cr, 91bl, 93tr, 93c, 100b, 101tl, 101tr, 101c, 105tl, 105c, 105cr, 106t, 107t, 107c, 109t, 109cr, 109b, 111t, 111b, 113tr, 113br, 115, 116b, 117tl, 117tr, 117c, 117br, 119tr, 121cl, 121c, 121br, 123tr, 123cl, 123cr; Mei Lim 4, 5, 12, 13, 14, 15, 20, 46t, 94t; Linden Artists/Shirley Felts cover/Jane Pickering 8–9, 42, 44b, 46b, 48, 50, 52, 54, 56, 58, 60, 62, 64b, 66, 68, 70, 72t, 73cr, 74, 76b, 78, 80, 82, 84, 86, 88, 90, 92, 94b, 96, 98t, 100t, 102, 104, 106b, 108, 110, 112, 114, 116t, 118, 120, 122, 124b/Joyce Tuhill 20, 21, 44t, 45bl, 64t, 69tr, 72b, 73cr, 76t, 77br, 89cl, 98b, 123tl, 124t. All other illustrations from *The Mitchell Beazley Pocket Guide to Mushrooms and Toadstools*.

The publishers wish to thank the following organisations and individuals for their kind permission to reproduce the following photographs in this book:

Biofotos/Heather Angel 27; A W Brand 37, 107; Stephen Gorton 11 cut-out, 12, 53r, 80; Thomas Laessøe 13, 62, 81, 92, 102, 104, 105, 111, 114, 120, 121, 122; Nature Photographers Ltd – Frank Blackburn 17b, 58, 63, 78/Brinsley Burbidge 20, 21b, 54/Robin Bush 17t/Keith Carlson 110/Andrew Cleave 10t, 18/John Doe 61/E A Janes 5b, 31/Mrs M E Hems 93/Paul Sterry cover, 4, 5t, 11t, 19, 41, 50, 53l, 56, 67, 91, 96/Anthony Wharton 52; Roger Phillips 66; Octopus Publishing 16; Alan Outen 21t, 33, 48, 70, 74, 86, 87, 88; Brian Spooner 10b, 11c, 11b, 42, 57, 68, 84, 108, 112, 118